Intelligence *for* Your Life

Intelligence *for* Your Life

POWERFUL LESSONS FOR PERSONAL GROWTH

JOHN TESH

THOMAS NELSON
Since 1798

NASHVILLE   DALLAS   MEXICO CITY   RIO DE JANEIRO   BEIJING

Published in Nashville, Tennessee, by Thomas Nelson. Thomas Nelson is a registered trademark of
Thomas Nelson, Inc.

Thomas Nelson, Inc., titles may be purchased in bulk for educational, business, fund-raising, or sales
promotional use. For information, please e-mail SpecialMarkets@ThomasNelson.com.

Unless otherwise noted, Scripture quotations are taken from the HOLY BIBLE: NEW INTERNA-
TIONAL VERSION® (NIV). © 1973, 1978, 1984 by International Bible Society. Used by permission
of Zondervan. All rights reserved.

Other Scripture quotations are from THE CONTEMPORARY ENGLISH VERSION (CEV). © 1991
by the American Bible Society. Used by permission. The Message (MSG) by Eugene H. Peterson. © 1993,
1994, 1995, 1996, 2000, 2001, 2002. Used by permission of NavPress Publishing Group. All rights
reserved. NEW AMERICAN STANDARD BIBLE® (NASB). © The Lockman Foundation 1960, 1962,
1963, 1968, 1971, 1972, 1973, 1975, 1977, 1995. Used by permission. THE NEW KING JAMES VER-
SION (NKJV). © 1982 by Thomas Nelson, Inc. Used by permission. All rights reserved.

Managing Editor: Jennifer McNeil
Page Design: Mandi Cofer

Library of Congress Cataloging-in-Publication Data
Tesh, John.
        Intelligence for your life : powerful lessons for personal growth / John Tesh.
            p. cm.
        ISBN 978-0-8499-2043-1 (hardcover)
            I. Success. 2. Conduct of life. 3. Success—Religious aspects—Christianity. 4. Tesh, John.
    I. Title.
    BJ1611.2.T43 2008
    650.1—dc22

                                                                                2007052509

Printed in the United States
08 09 10 11 12 QW 7 6 5 4 3 2 1

This book is dedicated to the three most inspiring people I know: Connie Tesh, Gib Gerard and Prima Tesh.

CONTENTS

Section Four: Take Care of Your Health

Section Five: Take Care of Business

Acknowledgments

This book would not have been possible without the remarkable people who have been so supportive during its creation. First of all to my wife, Connie, who has taught me well how to measure myself as a Godly man. Thank you, Connie, for your patience and for your devotion. Thanks also to my son, Gib, who continues to challenge me with his wit and brilliant insight. Gib, I will wait for you in heaven so we can spend our weekends watching Gladiator. Thank you, Prima Tesh, for taking a strong stand for Christ, for making me such a proud dad and for providing material for many of the great stories in this book.

This Intelligence for Your Life manuscript grew out of a concept for a radio show I created by the same name. The program would exist if not for the tireless work of Scotty Meyers and lead writer/producer Betsy Chase and her staff. Betsy, thank you for never compromising. Special thanks to Cindy Pearlman who took the lead on much of the research and direction for this project. Matt Baugher, I am grateful to you for believing that I could actually finish the manuscript. And thanks for the many chapter ideas. Jonathan Rogers; thank you for the 11th hour push and editing expertise and thanks to Jennifer McNeil for masterminding that finishing touch. And finally, to the millions of John Tesh Radio Show listeners: you encourage me every day with your emails and phone calls.

Welcome to *Intelligence* for *Your Life*

Let me start out by explaining this book was not my idea. It was a good idea—but it wasn't mine. It grew out of a couple of thousand encouraging e-mails from people just like you who listen to our radio show. The title comes from the radio program I created back in 2001, the *John Tesh Radio Show: Music and Intelligence for Your Life*.

You might say you're holding the print version of the *John Tesh Radio Show*. I fell in love with the medium of radio even before my broadcasting career began in 1973 at WKIX radio in Raleigh, North Carolina. Radio is truly a "theater of the mind," and I have always respected the way it can reach people in ways television never has and never will. After starting in radio, however, I got lured into the TV world. I enjoyed a wonderful career in local news, then network sports, then as a commentator for the Olympic Games, and finally as cohost of *Entertainment Tonight*. I left *Entertainment Tonight* in 1996 to follow my passion for playing concert piano, but I soon missed having a "voice" on the air.

> *"In this life we cannot do great things.*
> *We can only do small things with great love."*
> —MOTHER TERESA

I wanted to get back into radio, but I felt that between count-down shows and the mindless garbage that is so much drive-time radio, the medium was supersaturated. If I was going to get back into radio, I wanted to create something that was different, exciting, and useful—something with purpose. But how?

The answer was sleeping next to me. My wife, Connie Sellecca, is one of the most enlightened people I know. She is a great wife, mother, and actress; she runs her own skin-care company; and she is an information junkie! She's the person you want to visit with around the watercooler. She has seen the *Dateline* episode you missed. She has seen the *Today Show* twice (East Coast and West Coast feed) before most people have even gotten up in the morning. She has *Headline News* on in her office and *Fox News Radio* on in her car. At night it's either Discovery Channel or History Channel or both at once. She knows about every home inva-sion in Encino and the migration habits of the Australian red wattlebird. She guesses correctly when asked, "Where in the world is Matt Lauer?"

But Connie is human. She can't get to everything. On the floor by her side of the bed is a huge stack of magazines with little sticky notes marking articles she will "eventually" get to: *Prevention*, *Oprah*, *Better Homes and Gardens*—you name it.

Aha! I thought. That's it. I've got it! We'll create a radio program for this *woman. Someone who wants to be better at everything she does . . . who wants to be informed but doesn't have the time to get to all the great intelligence in this world.* And so from my wife's hunger to be as informed as possible—and from the stack of magazines with little yellow notes pasted on them—sprouted the original idea for the *Intelligence for Your Life* radio program—a program that offers answers to the big questions our listeners are asking:

- What does it mean to live an intelligent life?
- How can we practice it every day?
- How can we use this intelligence to set new goals in our lives and then come up against fear and doubt?
- What part does the "art of listening" play in everything we do?
- How does the power of forgiveness figure into the formula for creating passion and purpose in our everyday lives?

We started with six stations—and with the help of Scotty Meyers, Betsy Chase, Mike McVay, and a huge staff of very intelligent researchers—we have grown (at this writing) to three hundred affiliates. And while I originally intended the show to be for people like my wife, soon we were getting reactions from single men and women, from married couples listening together, from truck drivers, even from kids who now e-mail us every day with stories of how they stump their teachers with their new-found intelligence.

Our listeners have created our catchphrases for us:

"The more you listen, the more you know."

"We're here to make you the smartest person in the room."

"The 411 so your life never becomes a 911."

"Life coaching on the radio."

"If it doesn't move you forward in your life, you'll never hear it on the *John Tesh Radio Show*."

Soon we became known as the radio show that's safe for the whole family. As we say, "If it's not appropriate for a nine-year-old, you won't hear it on the *John Tesh Radio Show*."

As for me, I have the best job anyone could possibly have. I get to come to work every day and do five hours of radio that's all about training to be a better person. Then on weekends my band and I go out and meet the listeners as we perform concerts all over North America. Quick, somebody pinch me.

So what exactly does that have to do with this book? Well, as I mentioned earlier, this book wasn't my idea. But when a few thousand listeners keep e-mailing you saying, "Please turn this into a book!" or "Do you have some sort of a manual that's just like your show?" or simply "This would make a great book," it's a little hard to resist.

As you page through this book, understand that I am not a

therapist or a PhD I did not take a bunch of courses studying how to live a life of intelligence, purpose, and passion. But I do have some strong testimony in this area, because I have tried life both ways. I have lived life as a man fully alive, and I have lived life as a man just getting by. In other words, I've made the big mistakes. I can give witness to those mistakes, and hopefully you can learn from them with perhaps a bit less pain.

I have also spent the last five years or so connected to some of the finest thinkers in the world in the areas of interpersonal relationships, health and fitness, spiritual awareness, work life, business, and even pets. Take the best of that intelligence, pair it up with a good dose of my own story, and you have a good sense of what *Intelligence for Your Life* is.

So, here we go. It's time to step out of your old life and move into the one for which God created you. It's time to live an intelligent life!

As I am fond of saying on the radio show, "If it doesn't move you forward in your life, if it doesn't cause you to make a difference in someone else's life, you won't hear it here."

My biggest prayer for this book is that it will be useful to you. May God richly bless you.

John Tesh

LIVING YOUR LIFE
ON PURPOSE

I might as well start by being brutally honest: I spent the first forty years of my life living for *me*. Sure, I went to church. I even prayed. But when I prayed, I was always asking God to make sure he took care of *me*.

When I was growing up, I was very concerned about the state of *me*, and when I got to college, I went a little crazy because *I* wanted to feel good. I made all my decisions based on whether those decisions would make *me* more popular or desirable. After I graduated from college and got into the radio and television business, I worked hard so people would notice *me*. Then I switched jobs so employers would pay *me* more money that I could spend on *me*.

How exhausting!

Yes, the hedonistic, materialistic life will wear you out. If you have lived that life, you know that it is truly the road to hell. What's amazing to me is that God didn't just hit me with a stray bolt of lightning or run my Porsche into a semi. Seriously, the way I know there is a living God is the simple fact that I am still alive. I believe God had patience with me and actually put some thought into keeping me alive. Of course, there had to be some times when he and the angels had their doubts. I can just picture the angel Gabriel making a speech: "I mean, Lord, God, can I be brutally honest? Tesh is pretty much going for himself down there. Do you really think reading the celebrity birthdays is going to further your kingdom? For your Son's sake, God, he could have sponsored a few dozen of your hungry children with the money he just spent on a new sports car. Couldn't we just let him slip in the shower and move on?"

But God had another plan.

I'll never forget that day. It was May 1995. I was sitting in the Los Angeles Coliseum with eighty-thousand men at a Promise Keepers event, and Dr. Tony Evans came to the podium. He was angry. He was fired up. He took the stage with a purpose. He was sick and tired of men going through the motions in life and not taking charge in a world that needed men to be more like William Wallace and Maximus and less like Pee-Wee Herman.

"Come out!" Evans screamed. "Come out of the closet! Everyone else in this town has come out of the closet for one reason or another, but you 'good Christian men' are hiding in there with the door locked, cowering and refusing to take a stand for God. Come out! Come out and show yourselves." Evans stomped and prowled the stage. The veins in his neck expanded as he continued to shout us down. "Look at you! You're all undercover. You guys have gone CIA for God. You're 'secret agent

Christians.' Where are you when your children need you? Why do you refuse to lead your family? Men of God, show yourselves! Accept your purpose as godly men and act *now*, before it's too late! The world is waiting for you to come out of the closet and start living the life for which God made you. Come out of the closet!"

That was it. I was cooked. I can still hear those eighty-thousand voices ringing in my ears today. It was a thunderous, primal, earth-shattering scream. Eighty thousand men roared back their agreement with Dr. Evans as we all at once accepted our failings as men and embraced the need for rebirth, direction, and purpose. I've seen many Internet postings and blogs since that speech from men claiming it was the turning point in their lives. For me, it was conviction. For God, I'm sure it was the moment for which he had remained patient.

Men and women are hardwired by God to have a purpose, but we get distracted by the world and thus lose our way. Helen Keller said it best: "Many people have a wrong idea of what constitutes true happiness. It is not attained through self-gratification, but through fidelity to a worthy purpose." As Robert Byrne wrote, "The purpose of life is a life of purpose." And that purpose—the kind of purpose that actually changes lives—reaches outside the self. It goes beyond *me*. Look at Proverbs 19:21: "Many are the plans in a man's heart, but it is the LORD's purpose that prevails." We're always striving for some purpose. In the end, however, it's God's purpose that prevails. And it's a good thing too.

There has to be a reason my friend Rick Warren's book *The Purpose-Driven Life* has sold thirty million copies. We are a society hungry for direction. We seem a bit lost when it comes to figuring out which way to point our compass. Warren asks the challenging question, "What on earth are we here for?" It's the same question everybody asks at some point. Thankfully, he offers an answer: "You were made for a mission,"[1] according to one of his chapter titles. You aren't here just to wander around lost. And you aren't here simply to live for yourself.

> **DID YOU KNOW** *that the earth gets heavier each day? The extra weight is a result of meteoric dust settling on the planet.*

I love the way Eugene Peterson paraphrases Proverbs 11:28 in *The Message*: "A life devoted to things is a dead life, a stump; a God-shaped life is a flourishing tree." I look back at my life prior to encountering people like Tony Evans and Rick Warren, and it makes me sad. What caused me to spend so much of my personal inventory on earthly pleasures? What made me think it was possible to derive pleasure from being famous? Warren is fond of saying, "Between this day and the next you will give your life to something. The decision on what that will be will shape your destiny."[1]

Are you receiving this? Read it again: we will become what we worship. If all you think about is money, then your god is money. If all you think about is *People* magazine . . . well, there you go. At the writing of this chapter I am fifty-five years old.

Given the average life expectancy for someone like me (seventy-five years), I figure I have just about twenty years to go. That's twenty Christmases with my family. Twenty summer vacations. A little more than a thousand weekends.

When you see it laid out that way, it's a little scary. But it has also served to light me up and move me forward in my life. I know that I was made for a purpose. I also know that it took me a long time to figure that out. If you meet me in person, you'll see. I have purpose anxiety; I am anxious to make a difference before it's too late. I even have purpose now as I write this: to encourage you to catch my enthusiasm and not waste a precious moment that could be spent in service.

> I HAVE PURPOSE ANXIETY; I AM ANXIOUS TO MAKE A DIFFERENCE BEFORE IT'S TOO LATE.

Thomas Carlyle wrote, "The man without a purpose is like a ship without a rudder—a waif, a nothing, a no man." How do you determine your purpose in life? How do you live a "purpose-driven life"? As I'll illustrate in the next chapter, it has a lot to do with finding your passion in life and pursuing it. In many ways, that's what the rest of this book is about, so I won't attempt to summarize it here. However, I will say that living a life of purpose takes work, and it takes support. If you are surrounded right now with people who are not aligned with your new mission in life, it will be difficult. Part of living with purpose is learning to act immediately on the encouraging tug of your conscience. If you keep the company of people who constantly find a reason not to take action, then you will find it challenging to move forward into action yourself. If you spend your days in the company of joy suckers, you too will contract that horrible disease. Purpose-driven people encourage each other and stand shoulder to shoulder in battle.

Living with purpose, living intelligently, is a matter of vision. Like a football quarterback, when purpose-driven people look at the playing field, they don't see line markers and grass; they see opportunities for scoring touchdowns. When they see an opening, they call the appropriate play. They are active, not passive. They see the big picture, but instead of being intimidated they embrace the opportunity to make a difference.

Following is a compelling experience we had with our radio show listeners that perfectly illustrates what I mean about purpose-driven people seeing the field differently.

When Hurricane Katrina struck the Gulf Coast, we were all devastated by the pictures we saw on the news. We reported on the radio show the stories of loss and courage, and I made an effort to speak into the hearts of our listeners, encouraging them to find a way to help the victims. We put up links on our Web site to the Red Cross and many other relief organizations. We told the stories of human suffering. We did our part—or so we thought. But then the e-mails started pouring in. I was not prepared for the criticism they contained. For example:

Dear John Tesh,

You are always talking on your program about living outside yourself and about serving others and having purpose. How about *living* some of that talk yourself? My family and I live in Long Beach, Mississippi, and our town has been completely wiped out. Our home is gone, our school is gone, we're living in a tent—and all everyone keeps talking about is how bad it is over in New Orleans. Mr. Tesh, we need your help, and we need it now. No one has come to bring us aid. The government is nowhere to be found. You can help us. Please come and see for yourself how bad it is in Long Beach.

God bless you,

A Faithful Listener

I felt like such a jerk. The listener was right. I saw myself as one of those people who hears someone's terrible story of pain and suffering, then glibly says, "I'll pray for you," just before walking away from that person's suffering. Prayer is wonderful, but the Bible is pretty clear that faith without works is dead.

Within minutes of reading the e-mail, I had gathered up the radio show personnel to brainstorm, and I called our friends at Operation Blessing, a wonderful organization steered in the field by Bill Horn. Our family had traveled to Sri Lanka with Bill and Operation Blessing, and we knew they would be in the thick of the Katrina relief efforts. It turns out that Bill not only had relief workers on the ground in Long Beach, but also in Slidell,

Louisiana, another small town leveled by the hurricane. Operation Blessing is famous for finding opportunities the government misses and moving in with lightning speed. There aren't a lot of forms to fill out, they just start feeding people and setting up tent cities. I mentioned to Bill that one of my ideas was to hire a bunch of buses and move people out of the area. He said, "We tried that, John, but no one wants to leave. They are camping out in their front yards. They are afraid someone will loot what's left in their homes. What they really need is temporary housing, and for some reason FEMA is not sending motor homes or trailers. It's a mess."

And then it came to me. *We* can do this. *We* can use the radio show to raise money and purchase used travel trailers and motor homes. Then we'll drive them to the Gulf Coast and leave them for the families there. We'll call it the Katrina Convoy.

As usual, my awesome staff took one deep breath and we were on our way. Betsy wrote up promos for the radio show and started the fund-raising. Gib Gerard and Scott Cable began negotiating with trailer parks and individual owners to buy used trailers and motor homes. Dale Daniels at our Birmingham, Alabama affiliate made the deals for the trailer purchases. Mike Drolet created the logo and set up the Web site, and Scotty Meyers called all three hundred of our affiliates and had them promote the launch of the Katrina Convoy. Donations came pouring in from everywhere. When Sweetwater Sound and Manheim Steamroller heard that all the band instruments had been destroyed at Slidell High School, they donated hundreds of instruments—brass, woodwinds, keyboards. It was all just amazing. It was as if everyone had been sitting by the phone, waiting for us to ask them to jump in.

On Tuesday, October 11, 2005, the Katrina Convoy pulled out of the Riverchase Galleria parking lot in Birmingham. Our staff and radio show listeners traveled at the front in a tour bus. Above us, helicopter news crews tracked our progress live on the morning news. And seventy-five used motor homes and travel trailers packed with tools, musical instruments and bottled water (donated by listeners and sponsors) snaked their way along the interstate toward the Gulf Coast. Before we hit the road, two hundred elementary school kids painted each trailer with beautiful watercolor pictures and messages of hope. From the air, it looked like the Partridge Family had gone back on tour.

When we arrived, the mayors of Slidell and Long Beach were there to greet us. Later that day we all ended up in tears as we had an opportunity to visit with the families who would make these trailers their homes. At that moment I was instantly struck by my own personal reflection. What if I had never read that e-mail? What if Tony Evans hadn't screamed at me in the LA coliseum to "come out of the closet"? What if our radio show listeners hadn't held me accountable?

In our conference room at the *John Tesh Radio Show* offices there is a framed photo of one of the trailers from the convoy. It stands as a reminder to us all of how simple and how much fun living your life on purpose can be. On the side of the trailer, in little-kid watercolor writing, are the words "We Love You. Stay Strong!"

> *"Anytime you use your God-given abilities
> to help others, you are fulfilling your calling."*
> —RICK WARREN

The kind of intelligent life I'm talking about isn't rocket science. It does require, however, that you pay attention. It requires that you be intentional and proactive, willing to take control of the things you can control and let go of some things you can't. Most of all, it requires that you make choices—large and small—with a greater vision in mind. As I have learned from my radio listeners, there are a lot of people out there who are ready to live that way.

This book will show you how. It is organized in a way that will walk you step-by-step through a life of intelligence and purpose. After this introduction, the remaining sections look like this:

One: Find Your Passion
Two: Focus and Simplify
Three: Take Care of Your Relationships
Four: Take Care of Your Health
Five: Take Care of Business
Six: Trust God

It's pretty simple, really. You understand what you're passionate about. You focus on those things, trimming away the things that don't really matter (in other words, you simplify). You take care of your relationships, your health, and your work life. You trust God for the results. A life of intelligence is a life that's more purposeful, more effective, and happier. There's no reason you shouldn't have that kind of life.

Find Your Passion

Wherever you are right now in your life, there lives within you an urge to go deeper. To be useful. To be alive. When you resist that urge, you kill any chance of living a life of purpose.

LIVING ON PURPOSE

I love asking people big life questions. It's a hobby of mine. It doesn't always advance my friendships or win me new ones, but it can be wonderfully challenging nonetheless, for both the asker and the askee.

Here's my favorite question: "Tell me the deepest desire of your heart." You want to see someone frozen in his or her tracks? Just ask that question. And while you're at it, ask yourself. It is my opinion that very few of us find that deep desire within us. So each day we pursue *happiness* instead of desire—what our *hearts* desire. If someone asks you to state the deepest desire of your heart and you don't have an answer, there's a good chance

"TELL ME THE DEEPEST DESIRE OF YOUR HEART."

you're living your life merely as a *reaction* to what happens to you. You know, stimulus response. Rats do that; ring bell, get cheese.

The successful people I have interviewed and met in my travels all share these important distinctions: They *know* what they desire.

They are sure of it. They live it intentionally. They know what makes them come alive, and therefore they know where their compass points. Sadly, it took me years to accept my heart's deepest desire. Notice I said "accept." We all are born with our own personal desires, but a great many of us spend our lives denying those desires and instead go with what the world would have us do. Or maybe we just eventually give up and distract (or drown) ourselves in video games, text messaging, shopping, food, alcohol, or some other self-medicating habit.

> **DID YOU KNOW** *that the number of cars on the planet is increasing three times faster than the population growth?*

So, what is your deepest desire? It's a question first posed to me by John Eldredge in his book *Wild at Heart*. What is that one thing, when you are doing it, that causes you to lose track of time? What do you do that gives you great pleasure and a sense of purpose without regard to monetary reward? If you won the lottery, or if you had only one year to live, what would you do?[1]

Before you answer, let me hit you with a quote from author Harold Thurman that I often have playing in my head: "Don't ask yourself what the world needs. Ask yourself what it is that makes you come alive, and then go do that. Because what the world needs are men and women who have come alive."

That's deep. It begs the question, why don't we do what makes us come alive? How have we missed the deepest desire of our hearts?

First, let me say it's not entirely our fault. It's a big world out there, and that world is always trying to conform us to it. We've heard it a thousand times, "Be in the world but not of it." But it's hard to live in it without becoming part of it. Reality shows, magazines, and Internet sites bombard us with the idea that celebrity is the highest good. Kids get the message that a Mercedes-Benz is the symbol of a life well lived, that earthly pleasure is the best happiness we can hope for in life. The world—money, parents, friends, fame—can easily cloud the vision of what God originally planted in our hearts.

RANDOM INTELLIGENCE: *If you want to reduce the amount of time you spend watching TV, switch it off during meal times. Watching the tube while eating can add an extra 70 minutes to your viewing time.*

When we're young it's especially hard because our parents and relatives can't help but get involved in helping us select a career. We ask ourselves what the world needs. Or maybe we don't even ask anything that deep. Maybe we ask, "What will make my parents proud and happy?" or "What will get me lots of money and fame and a Mercedes?" In any case, some of us were talked out of choosing what makes us come alive. But here's the truth: our deepest desire will eventually seek its rightful place in our life. Like a bottle of cola forgotten in the freezer, like a ticking time bomb, there will be an explosion. It's only a matter of time.

If you had seen me as a grade school child, you would have

seen a boy keen on defining his life with music and live performance. I played in the high school band and orchestra. I stayed up late nights charting chords off of Jimi Hendrix records. I was in two garage bands. I snuck into clubs to see live bands. I built Heathkit amateur electronic kits and used them to broadcast into my parents' car radios.

> *"There couldn't be a society of people who didn't dream. They'd be dead in two weeks."*
>
> —William Burroughs

But my mom and dad were convinced, like many baby boomer parents, that music was not a respectable, viable vocation. So they "strongly encouraged" me to apply to college to study textile chemistry, my father's occupation. My dad had carved out a wonderful living working for Hanes, and I had worked during the summer months in the Hanes dye mill. So joining Hanes seemed like the logical, sensible choice. Sound familiar?

I enrolled in North Carolina State and attended classes on surface-active agents, statistics, and weave factors. I was a C-minus student. At night, I would sneak into the music building's piano practice rooms, and for hours I played songs by Yes and Emerson, Lake and Palmer. Eyes closed, I lost myself in what had always been my deepest desire.

In January of my sophomore year, my friend and soccer

teammate Steve Thomas suggested that I might enjoy a brand-new elective course at the university, Radio-Television 101. From the first day in class, I was a whirling dervish of creativity—writing copy, shooting camera, editing videotape, and then scoring it all with a beat-up Moog synthesizer. On weekends I took a hosting shift at the campus radio station, WKNC-FM. I was hooked. I didn't even tell my parents I had signed up for that first class, by the way. When they finally found out that I had switched my major, it got pretty ugly.

The short version of the rest of this story? I embarked on a professional career in music and television that led me through local TV news, network sports, and a music recording and scoring career. I ended up hosting *Entertainment Tonight*, and today I'm a syndicated radio host and touring musician. That's a pretty varied résumé. As you may have noticed, it doesn't include any mention of textiles.

WHAT THE WORLD NEEDS IS *YOU, FULLY ALIVE.*

I was fortunate. I don't know what would have happened if Steve hadn't suggested the TV and radio course. I'm grateful he did.

So, what is the deepest desire of your heart? What is it that makes *you* come fully alive? Ask yourself that question—and when you have the answer, go do that, because what the world needs is *you, fully alive.*

Big Life Question: Do my parents still know best?

You need to figure out what's right for you despite what your parents think. Maybe they don't think you should take a career break or move to another state to be with your girlfriend, but if you feel strongly about what you're doing—and you've looked at the consequences— make your own decisions. My parents insisted I would starve to death as a musician. I took their advice and took chemistry courses in college. I wasted valuable time because my parents (and they were great parents) didn't really understand how serious I was about a career in music, radio, and television.

Big Life Question: Do I know what my passions are?

If your answer to this Big Life Question is "No," or "I'm not sure," then ask yourself four more questions:

1. What makes me feel most energized and excited?
2. What do I want to be known as?
3. What could I talk about nonstop?
4. Which activities do I get so caught up in that time just flies?

PASSION AND ACTION

In order to become consistently passionate about your life, you must do more than merely "dream" your passion. This world is full of people who have dreams of playing Carnegie Hall, of running a marathon, of owning their own business. The difference between the people who make it across the finish line and everyone else is one simple thing: an action plan.

> *"Courage is being scared to death—but saddling up anyway."*
> —JOHN WAYNE

You can pray all you want. You can dream day and night. But if you don't come up with a plan, you're dead in the water. I remember how excited I was when I decided to record my first album. I worked for hours on all the songs and hired musicians to fill out the tracks. I even found a graphic artist to create a compelling piece of cover art. The work, *Music from the Tour de*

France, was a soundtrack I composed for CBS-TV.

And I had what I thought was

GETTING EXCITED ABOUT AN
IDEA IS NOT MUCH OF A PLAN.

a brilliant plan. I would finish
the project, then take it to a record company to get signed as a
recording artist. Then the records would go into stores and I
would sell thousands. Since twenty million people saw me
every night cohosting *Entertainment Tonight*, the record companies
would see a wonderful opportunity for free promotion and
staggering record sales.

I still have the rejection letters on my wall. Warner
Brothers. Arista (Clive Davis himself). Columbia. They all
said it different ways, but they all said the same thing: "Sorry,
not interested." What went wrong? Getting excited about an
idea is not much of a plan. I was a victim of my own feelings of
entitlement. Plus, my plan was based on a flawed formula: CD
recording + John Tesh = cover of *Rolling Stone*. Not much
"action" in the plan.

I hope this retelling of my mistakes might save you some time
and pain. But the story doesn't end there. I went to David
Michaels, the producer of the Tour de France and a believer in
the music, and asked for his advice. Instead of giving me advice,
he began to ask me some tough questions:

David: Why did you create this album?
Me: Because I am passionate about this race and the music.
David: Who could you see wanting to own this soundtrack?

Me: Viewers of the Tour de France coverage, people who ride bikes, and people who like intense workout music in their Walkman.

David: Where are these people?

Me: At home watching the tour, in bike stores, reading cycling magazines, and perhaps in health clubs.

Within an hour we had come up with a plan that included everything except being signed to a record company or having my soundtrack in record stores.

This action plan included direct response (infomercial) TV advertising on the CBS race coverage (I put it on my credit card), placement in bike stores (on consignment), videotapes of bike-racing footage set to my music sent to key stores, revenue-sharing deals with two bike magazines in return for interviewing me, and hundreds of personal visits by yours truly to local bike races with just a card table, albums, and flyers.

There was no MTV video, no radio play, and no Grammy nomination. This was a true action plan: it included hand-to-hand combat. There was nothing very glamorous here.

For the next three months I fulfilled requests for ten

> **DID YOU KNOW** *that if you yelled for eight years, seven months, and six days, you would have produced enough sound energy to heat one cup of coffee? You would probably be hoarse too.*

thousand CDs and cassettes out of my Los Angeles apartment and collected $122,000 in net profits. Through the process, I harvested the names and addresses of about six thousand fans who were ready for album number two when it came out. It took hard work, risk, and action.

In my office is a framed poster of that first Tour de France cover. Next to it are posters of CDs and DVDs that became Public Television specials and gold albums that were all created and marketed with that same basic plan: Dream + Passion + Action Plan = SUCCESS.

> DREAM + PASSION + ACTION PLAN = SUCCESS.

Now it's up to you. I have no business degree. I have no marketing background . . . just the belief that out there somewhere are people who will catch the joy that I have for my music or our radio show or this book. And I have finally come to the end of ego and realized that I actually have to put my own shoe leather to the ground and do the work.

> *"I dream, therefore I exist."*
> —J. AUGUST STRINDBERG

I've met enough people at my concerts and read enough letters and e-mails to know that there are millions of you out there right now who are sitting on a dream. Perhaps you've *already* created something incredible. I know, it's a unique idea for a restaurant chain, a new way to bring music into nursing homes, a hip-hop dance troupe that will tour the world, a new small group at your church that will feed the homeless, an extra four hours in your day to homeschool your children, a qualifying time for the Boston Marathon, or a record night of fundraising at your kid's school.

Stop sitting on it. It ain't gonna hatch on its own.

And let me leave you with a secret. Whatever you are about to do, whatever action you will next take to realize your dream, it's been done before. Maybe not exactly what *you're* about to do, but close. Do your research. Ask experienced people what they would do. Get passionate, and then *take action*.

Big Life Question: Do I really need to be richer?

According to the Consumer Credit Counseling Service, you don't need to win the lottery to change your financial situation. They recommend putting away $80 a week for five years. You'll have a nest egg of $20,000 when you're done. And to motivate you to save, have a goal, such as buying a new car or putting a down payment on a home.

THE MANAISSANCE

I've already mentioned that life-changing moment at the Los Angeles Coliseum when Tony Evans challenged eighty thousand men to "come out of the closet" and get passionate about their God-given responsibility to stand up and act like men. I've never seen such passion. It was as if I was coming alive and watching thousands of men come alive beside me.

> DID YOU KNOW *that one out of every four dogs in animal shelters is a purebred? So save yourself some money and save a life. If there's a specific breed you're interested in, there's a decent chance you will find the perfect dog at a shelter.*

This is a chapter especially for men (though women readers are welcome to read it, of course). For the last few decades, we men have had a hard time "being men" in this culture. We've been tamed, rendered harmless, our true passions squelched in favor of a sensitivity that, frankly, isn't always sincere. If men are going to pursue their passion, they're going to have to start by reclaiming their masculinity.

Believe me, I know all about it. I live with three females—my wife Connie, my daughter Prima, and Lucy the dog. I am surrounded by women. If I am not constantly vigilant, I will end up sitting around the kitchen table talking about the color of drapes, or worse, sitting in a nail salon. Actually, it's always been that way for me—the women, women everywhere syndrome. I have two older sisters: Bonnie (eleven years older) and Mary Ellen (nine years older). When I was born, I think my mom must have said, "Hey girls, just take care of him, will ya?"

AS AN "ONLY" CHILD WITH THREE "MOTHERS," I FOUND MYSELF DESPERATE FOR MANLY ADVENTURES.

And so as an "only" child with three "mothers," I found myself desperate for manly adventures. My dad recognized the danger here. He had been raised on a farm in rural North Carolina, and he realized that a young boy in the house with three women, growing up in the suburbs of Long Island, needed a regular dose of testosterone. So this city boy spent every summer in Rural Hall, North Carolina, bunking with Grandma and Grandpa Tesh.

DID YOU KNOW *that you can tell whether a horse is male or female by looking at its teeth? Most males have 40 teeth, while females have only 36.*

Since Percy Tesh (Grandpa) was not all that interested in the mechanics of kickball and Little League, he proceeded to teach me the things he felt a "real man" needed to learn: how to pick corn; how to slop the hogs and hang and dry tobacco; how to pick off a watermelon-eating crow with a hipshot from a 12-gauge; how to catch and clean a striped bass with a twenty-foot line and hula-popper lure. We woke with the morning sun. We hit the sack an hour after sundown. No TV. No telephone. We ate what we raised and only stopped working to drink from the well. We walked two miles to the country store for supplies and said our prayers at every meal. And once, when I sassed Grandma, Percy taught me how to cut the proper-sized switch from the tree behind the barn, thus insuring that "yes 'um" would be my future reply to any requests by Grandma.

> **RANDOM INTELLIGENCE:**
> *If you want someone to do a favor for you, use the word* because *when you ask him or her—as in, "I need you to help me* because.*" Studies show that using this word increases the odds that the other person will help you.*[2]

Sure, I would have preferred spending my summers scarfing down Good Humors and hanging out at the Garden City pool, but looking back on my experiences "down on the farm" I realize that I was living in a man's world, and that in those moments I was alive and purposeful.

One of my all-time favorite authors is John Eldredge, who wrote the book *Wild at Heart*. The subtitle is *Discovering the Secret of a Man's Soul*. In his book, Eldredge endeavors to help men rescue their God-given hearts and to embrace their masculinity and true calling. Eldredge writes, "Capes and swords, camouflage, bandannas, and six shooters—these are the *uniforms* of boyhood. Little boys yearn to know they are powerful."[3] Brilliant! And one of the reasons John's book is a huge bestseller is that it resonates so deeply with men like me. Why do you think we men love the movies *Braveheart* or *Gladiator* or even *Die Hard* (the first one only)? We are hardwired by God to act heroically. But we live in a world today that handcuffs big brave men and seeks to make them shrink quietly from confrontation by telling them to "Get in touch with your feelings" or "Control yourself."

> *"The kingdom of heaven suffers violence,*
> *and violent men take it by force."*
> —Matthew 11:12 NASB

Cinderella Man. Spartacus. Now those are movies that celebrate real men. Eldredge points out that no matter what your woman tells you, she also is hardwired—to be *won* in battle. You want a purpose and a passion? A mission? There is one for you. Win your woman in battle.

One of the manliest men I know is our son, Gib. I'll never forget one evening in September of 2007 when we had Gib and his wife and some friends over for dinner. We live on the side of a mountain surrounded by all kinds of animals. Raccoons, deer, bobcats, and hundreds of coyotes that wander all over our property. For the last few months, the coyotes had been getting bolder than ever. Not only did our daughter have a face-to-face encounter, but one large animal even ran into the house to grab our terrier, Lucy. Something had to be done. As we discussed the problem over dinner, it finally became clear to Gib and me that we men must take matters into our own hands.

> "Without a great battle in which a man can live and die,
> the fierce part of his nature goes underground and sort of
> simmers there in a sullen anger that seems to have no reason."
> —JOHN ELDREDGE

I'll dispense with the boring particulars and just tell you that the next weekend, four of us men camped out at the foot of our hill with a shotgun, two giant knives, three slingshots, night-vision goggles, and a crossbow (an homage to our favorite medieval films). We surrounded our position with twenty pounds of raw hamburger meat and thirty cans of dog food. I was in charge of making wounded animal sounds. It was incredible. No one spoke for hours. We just sat and waited until sunrise with our weapons at the ready. No cell phones. No e-mail. No golf clubs. No women. Just testosterone.

I'M SURE THE COYOTES WERE HIDING IN THE BUSHES LAUGHING HYSTERICALLY.

I'm sure the coyotes were hiding in the bushes laughing hysterically, but no matter. We were men on a mission to protect our womenfolk—and Lucy the dog. And even though no shots were fired and no arrows flew, I must tell you it was wildly energizing, and I swear I even saw a new twinkle in my wife's eye when I returned the next morning. A man will always need a battle to fight and a beauty to rescue. It's the natural order of the world.

And it would appear that the art of being a man is making a comeback. The book *The Alphabet of Manliness* made it to the top of the *New York Times* best-seller list. The book is a compilation of "manly tips," like how to throw a punch properly, and why men should wear flannel and be proud. A decade or so ago, the ideal man was Tom Hanks—the guy with a soft side who doesn't mind wearing his heart on his sleeve. To picture the *new* ideal man, think Russell Crowe—the tough guy who might show his

> **DID YOU KNOW** *that dogs' sense of smell is one of the keenest in nature? Humans might smell a pot of stew cooking on the stove, but a dog can distinguish the smells of each individual ingredient, from the beef to the potatoes.*

feelings, but only after he has claimed victory on the battle-field. That's the *new* definition of manliness, or rather, the new old definition.

The *Boston Globe* even gave the new trend a name: Manaissance—like Renaissance. And basically, it means macho is making a comeback. Supporters of the Manaissance point out that we shouldn't be too concerned about what kind of man *women* want these days. That's how we ended up with the sensitive guy who wears moisturizer and designer jeans, who is now going out of fashion.

No amount of "de-manning" of the English language—from "chairman" to "chairperson," from "mankind" to "human-kind"—is going to change the fact that there are big differences between the sexes. And those differences should be celebrated. As the French say, *Vive la différence!* It's time men reclaimed their manliness.

> *"Courage is contagious. When a brave man takes
> a stand, the spines of others are stiffened."*
> —Billy Graham

What is a man these days? A real man is chivalrous, mature, and emotionally robust. He protects and provides for his wife and family. He is modest, doesn't wear his heart on his sleeve, and is basically the "go-to" guy who'd build a shelter and forage for food if you were shipwrecked on an island. And you ladies who are reading this, I challenge *you*: Encourage your guy to be manly. Celebrate his desire to lead. And moms and teachers, don't forget that boys and girls are profoundly different.

Eldredge points out what a horrible mistake it is to emascu-late young boys by constantly telling them, "Don't jump on the furniture." "Don't climb that tree." "Don't be so noisy." Of course, boys need boundaries. But they also need a mountain to climb and a battle to fight. I know it seems it would be easier if they would just sit down and be quiet and stop being so, well, boyish. But that's not really what you want for them. That's not who God made them to be. So be patient with the boys in your life, including the ones who are grown up!

> **DID YOU KNOW** *that ants can't chew their food? Instead, they move their jaws sideways, like scissors, to extract the juices from the food.*

A Passion for Service

I grew up in a household that was very performance-oriented. My dad was vice president of Hanes; my mom was a registered nurse. Our house was driven by report cards, piano recitals, Boy Scout merit badges, and the pride of brand-new aluminum siding. My dad, John Sr., was a self-made man who commanded troops in Okinawa in World War II. He grew up on a farm, and with no college education he rose to the top and bought his family a home in prestigious Garden City on Long Island. Our success, as a family and personally, was measured in dollars and cents and wall plaques.

> *"You can tell what they are by what they do."*
> —Matthew 7:16 cev

Then there was the other side of the family—our cousins from North Carolina who served in Liberia with the Peace

Corps. I actually remember a few dinner conversations when they were referred to as the "hippies" of the family. I suspect that the unspoken opinion among our family was that they joined the Peace Corps because they couldn't get jobs. I carried that ridiculous mantra in my heart for most of my life. But what I now recall is that Don, Joy, and Leslie Tesh were some of the happiest people I knew. They always had time to speak with me as a little kid. They seemed so relaxed and content. And they had amazing stories to tell about digging wells and creating gardens and building homes for people a world away who had none of these things. Up until then the only mission lesson I had received was at our dinner table: "Clean your plate. People in Africa are starving."

> *"One thing I know: the only ones among you who will be really happy are those who have sought and found how to serve."*
> —ALBERT SCHWEITZER

The fact is that we were designed to serve. God planted in us a conscience and a desire to love others. But somewhere along the way the world grabs hold of us and our hearts grow selfish. Mine sure did. The *aha* moment for me did not come until someone handed me Rick

GOD PLANTED IN US A CONSCIENCE AND A DESIRE TO LOVE OTHERS.

Warren's *The Purpose-Driven Life.* This book is basically the rudder that began to steer my ship. It is, of course, rife with scripture, but it also contains brilliant how-to chapters that spell it all out, just the way a guy needs it.

Soon, I was reading everything I could find on mission trips and service. Our researchers on the radio show found hundreds of studies on the power of serving others and its effect on blood pressure, longevity, and even business growth. We broadcast reports from respected learning institutions on how volunteerism helps people live longer and have stronger immune systems, fewer heart attacks, higher self-esteem, and a deeper sense of purpose in their lives. We also uncovered many studies showing that businesses with a culture of volunteerism grow faster, keep their employees longer, and form stronger relationships with their key business partners.

> *"Man is to be found in reason, God in the passions."*
> —G. C. LICHTENBERG

I have quoted studies proving that volunteering can play a role in increasing your overall sense of well-being, alleviating chronic pain, and even reducing depression. Peggy Thoits, professor of sociology at Vanderbilt University, studied how volunteering affected six different aspects of well-being. The study divided 3,617 respondents into two groups: those who volunteered, and those who did not. Comparisons were then made for levels of happiness, life satisfaction, self-esteem, sense of control over life, physical health, and depression. According to Dr. Thoits, "People of all ages who volunteered were happier and experienced better physical health and less depression."[4] In another study, Boston College's Paul Arnstein and his colleagues evaluated the effects of volunteering on chronic pain patients. Their findings show that pain, depression, and disability decreased after volunteering. The researchers note that the participants reported themes of "making a connection" and having "a sense of purpose" when volunteering.[5]

> FINDINGS SHOW THAT PAIN, DEPRESSION, AND DISABILITY DECREASED AFTER VOLUNTEERING.

By now you get the picture. Living a servant's life—even if just on weekends—is the best longevity pill you could possibly swallow. And I can tell you from personal experience, service draws amazing people to you. After my family and I traveled to Sri Lanka post-tsunami, and following our radio show's "Katrina Convoy," in which we brought temporary housing to help hurricane victims, our radio show listeners responded by mounting their own service and relief efforts. Our sponsors have funded many other service projects with us, and our opportunities to reach even more people in need have grown tenfold. And the best part of all? There are thousands of great organizations that have already put together plans that you and your family can plug into.

It's not all about building stuff or traveling to foreign countries. Can you read aloud? Do you have a car? Can you cook, plant a garden, do card tricks, play an instrument? Do you have a cute dog or a child who plays the violin? There are people who can use your help within a five-mile radius of where you are standing right now.

So don't over-think this. If you do, you'll think the life out of it. Go with your heart. Go to your bathroom mirror right now and do what I did. Write in black magic marker: "Today I will make a plan to serve others." It will take more effort to wash it off than it will to make a phone call or surf the Web and find out how to make it happen.

And here's one more plus: if you're single and looking to meet someone, imagine the type of person you'll meet in an organization that helps others. At www.tesh.com, we've even started a movement that can get you started. It's called Intelligent Kindness. You can also find different opportunities at the Web site of the International Volunteer Programs Association (www.volunteerinternational.org), which lists different volunteer organizations. When you do start serving or start a new project, call me on our hotline number at the radio show—1-866-865-TESH (8374)—and tell me what you are doing so we can encourage others.

Focus and Simplify

Life pulls us in a thousand different directions at once. Technology's promise to make life simpler has backfired in a big way. Pursuing your passion requires that you focus in a world that teems with distractions. To do that, you're going to have to simplify. Get rid of some things that are cluttering up your life and sapping away your energy, resources, and attention.

The Power of Focus

For about ten years of my life I worked as an announcer for CBS Sports and then NBC Sports. It was an amazing time for me because I was hired to cover all those events that you don't read about on the American newspaper sports pages. I never reported on football, basketball, or golf. My beat was gymnastics, figure skating, bike racing, speed skating, and downhill skiing. Those are some of the sports that Europeans love most; working over there I felt like an expatriate sports announcer.

Every four years, of course, we Americans go nuts for ice dancing and the giant slalom and curling and wrestling. When the Olympics come around, everybody becomes a temporary expert on the biathlon ("It's all in the breathing . . ."), and the luge ("He didn't keep his feet together; it cost him at least two tenths . . ."), and they soak up the biographies of athletes who, up until then, had labored in obscurity.

One of the best things about announcing the Games and many World Championships is that I lived with these athletes and their teams for months at a time. You would never get that kind of access to NBA or NFL players. And so I came to know them and their families and their passion for their sport. I've had dinner with French Tour de France champion Bernard Hinault at his home; I've skied with Austria's Olympic downhill champion Franz Klammer, and I've traveled all over Europe with gymnast Bart Conner and speedskater/cyclist Eric Heiden. Why am I name-dropping? Because I want to give credibility to what I am about to share with you. Every one of these world-class athletes shares something that you and I can use to take us to greatness in everything we do: *focus*.

> WHAT DISTINGUISHES THOSE WHO GO ON TO BECOME CHAMPIONS IS THE POWER OF FOCUS.

Focus is a wonderful thing to watch. There are plenty of incredibly talented downhill racers in the world, just as there are thousands of brilliant kids graduating Ivy League schools every year. What distinguishes those who go on to become champions is the power of focus.

I will always have burned into my memory the image of Franz Klammer just before he stepped into the starting gate to win the Kitzbuehl downhill—helmet on, eyes closed, hands weaving in the air as he ran the course in his mind. Before the gate opened, you could see the whole race in his face; you could watch the course come alive just by following his hands. Then his name blared forth from the speakers, and in moments he was out of the gate, attacking that same course—this time with his eyes open, at sixty-five miles an hour on a pair of skis.

Cyclists, gymnasts, divers. The great ones all prepare with the same routine. Greg Louganis had done the dive a thousand times, but he never lost the desire and discipline to stay focused. It's why so many football quarterbacks are also straight-A students. It's why many ex-athletes become successful announcers and businesspeople: they know the power of focus, and they practice it in everything they do. They never take their eyes off the prize.

THE GREAT ONES ALL PREPARE WITH THE SAME ROUTINE.

On the other hand, on any given day you can see what happens when people (or companies) lose focus. Company X sells the best hamburger in town. They get bought by a bigger company, XX, who takes them nationwide and expands their menu to include everything from salad niçoise to donuts and ribs. The hamburger fans get confused and start going elsewhere for their burgers. Tea Company Y wants to move their stock price up and decide they can do that by launching more flavored iced teas, so they add ten new flavors. Consumers get so rattled trying to make a decision at the grocery store they just buy a diet soda instead. Mercedes stands for luxury. BMW is the "ultimate driving machine." Volvo stands for safety. But when these brands have gotten lured into expanding or changing their focus, the results have been disastrous.

> DID YOU KNOW *that the corneas in your eyes have no blood supply? The cornea takes in oxygen directly from the air.*

Before we launched the *John Tesh Radio Show*, I made a commitment that it would be about intelligence for your life—all the information you need to be the smartest person in the room. That's it. No jokes. No silly humor. No stunts. Every day for five hours our mission would be to connect our listeners to the information they need to be better at everything. We vowed to be the nation's personal life coach.

DID YOU KNOW *that an eel can survive for 48 hours out of water? That's because an eel's skin is full of oil, which keeps it moist.*

At first, I got all kinds of advice. *Intelligence for Your Life* is too long a name. Take more listener phone calls; play more music; talk less. I heard it all. At this writing, the program is on more than three hundred radio stations around the country and is the highest rated independent radio show in North America. No brag, just fact. And I am convinced the reason it is so successful is because I read books like *Focus* by Al Ries and *Differentiate or Die* by Jack Trout and put their advice into practice. Those books share the same strong message: Be different. Be focused.

MULTITASKING WILL KILL YOUR FOCUS.

Today, right now, your focus is being challenged more than ever before. Multitasking will kill your focus. The lure of money will cause you to lose your focus. And sleep deprivation will also ruin any chance you have of staying on course.

And guess what? You need focus in everything you do. Have

you ever been in a discussion with your spouse and lost focus? Have you ever reached down to grab a french fry that dropped on the floorboard of your car? Losing focus can kill you. But each day we seem to lose a little more focus in everything we do. We pack our schedules with nonsense that leaves us exhausted and confused. We overschedule our kids with far too many activities. We have become reactors to way too many stimuli.

> *"In character, in manners, in all things,*
> *the supreme excellence is simplicity."*
> —HENRY WADSWORTH LONGFELLOW

Our biggest problem is that our "focus muscles" have atrophied. We think growth comes only through change, so we change everything even if it's already perfect. It's true enough that we need to be open to change. But it takes time to get things right. If everything is always changing for no good reason, how will we ever manage to perfect the latest change?

So what can we do to break the cycle? Following are a few ideas based on advice from many experts we have had on the show.

Practicing the
Art of Focus

Write down on three index cards at least two goals that you would like to complete during the next month. They could be anything. But you must write them down, and each time you see them you must speak them aloud. This is so your brain will both hear and see your goal. Examples:

"I will lose five pounds in one month by walking ten more minutes every day."

"I will read to my daughter every night before she goes to bed, even if it's just one page."

"I will smile at every customer in line and ask them if they are having an 'awesome day.'"

"I will raise the ratings in our three lowest markets by personally e-mailing listeners and asking them to tell their friends to listen."

Tape the cards to your computer at work, to the dashboard in your car, and to your bathroom mirror. And don't forget the part about speaking your goals out loud. That's important.

Whenever you start to lose focus on your goal (watching too much TV, surfing the Web, etc.), ask yourself this question: *What am I doing right now that is bringing me closer to my goal?* I'm not suggesting that you become obsessed, but you must monitor your focus to make sure that your life goals are front and center in your mind.

When you reach those two goals, add two more, then two more, and so on until the practice of focus becomes second nature. In an unfocused world, we must constantly retrain ourselves in the art of concentrated focus.

RANDOM INTELLIGENCE:
If you smoke a pack of cigarettes a day, and you quit, you'll save $1,500 a year. And the day you quit smoking your health will start improving.

This last one is aimed at me, but I will share it with you. Don't check your e-mail nearly as often as you do now; resist the temptation to stop what you're doing every time you hear that *ding!* For a start, wait fifteen minutes between each check of your e-mail inbox, and build up from there. Yeah, I know, I start to get the shakes too. But if you practice that technique for twenty-one days (the length of time it takes to break a habit), it will become second nature. Many experts have come on our program to tell us that every time you stop what you are doing to answer the e-mail *ding*, it takes at least ten minutes to completely recover and return to the task at hand.

I have one last bit of advice about focus: if you get derailed on your road to a more focused life, just shake it off and get started again. Remember our hero in this story, Franz Klammer?

Yes, he was focused. Yes, he was fearless. And yes, he is one of the greatest and most decorated ski racers of all time. But Franz Klammer also had days when he crashed headfirst into a snowdrift at sixty miles per hour. I can still remember one of the postrace interviews I did with Klammer following one of his spectacular crashes. He told me in that broken English of his, "You know, John, today here [pointing to his head] was no good. Tomorrow, it will be a good day for me."

JUST SHAKE IT OFF AND GET STARTED AGAIN.

CRUSH YOUR
BAD HABITS

To a large extent, developing focus is a matter of getting rid of bad habits and replacing them with good habits. That's not easy to do. If your habits were easy to change, well, they wouldn't be called habits. There's one fact to keep in mind as you struggle to change your habit: it takes about twenty-one days to form or break a bad habit.

Twenty-one days. This fact makes two things crystal clear:

First, we build our bad habits by being sloppy and inattentive to bad behavior for three weeks.

Second, we usually quit trying before we break the habit.

Most of the studies I have reported on the radio show recommend not just quitting "cold turkey" when it comes to your bad habit. It helps tremendously if you are able to substitute another action for the offending behavior. For example:

IT TAKES ABOUT TWENTY ONE DAYS TO FORM OR BREAK A BAD HABIT.

→ *My problem:*

I have had the terrible habit of checking my e-mails repeatedly while hosting the radio show. When we go to commercial, immediately I check my e-mail. Maybe I'll get something from my bank about a pension plan. Maybe it's yet another "exclusive offer" for some product or service I don't need. Or maybe it actually is something important. That's not the point. The point is that in two seconds, I'm completely derailed from the task at hand. While I'm doing the show, my heart and mind are supposed to be devoted to the next bit of relationship intelligence or the next health tip.

→ *My solution:*

I've replaced my e-mail checks with ten push-ups. I'm not kidding. It has worked wonders. It's simple: when the urge strikes to check e-mail, I hit the floor. Believe me, I'm not a big fan of push-ups; that's part of the reason my habit-breaking plan has worked for me. I'm twenty-one days into my plan, and my attention is razor sharp. By the way, I do check my e-mail later when it's appropriate and it doesn't distract my attention away from the major task at hand.

I also recommend rewarding yourself for breaking a habit. Let's say you're giving up your soda habit, which is basically just empty calories and sugar. If you've gone five days without a soda, treat yourself to dinner at your favorite restaurant. I haven't had my daily glass of wine for nineteen days as of this writing.

(I felt I was setting a bad example for my kids.) I just treated myself to a half pint of ColdStone's coffee ice cream to celebrate. Get it? Replace the bad behavior, reward yourself with milestone treats, and don't forget the twenty-one-day rule.

DID YOU KNOW *that one of the major ingredients in ice cream is air? Without it, ice cream would be very hard—similar to an ice cube—and difficult to eat. So air is incorporated into ice cream during the stirring process.*

Oh, and before I forget: to tackle something horrendously difficult like smoking, therapists recommend you tell everyone you know that you are trying to quit and ask them to help you. Also, try to do it with a friend. There's strength in numbers.

Big Life Question: What am I worried about?

Do you find that worry kills your ability to focus throughout the day? I've done stories about how therapists treat chronic, habitual worriers. As it turns out, the brain can't handle worrying and reading out loud simultaneously. Therapists teach their patients to read aloud whenever they feel a worrying episode coming on. So next time you're fretting over something, pick up a book or a magazine and start reading out loud. It will banish the worry.

Leave Room
for Cream

Of all the topics we research for our radio program, stress is probably the easiest one to find information about. For decades, scientists and physicians have searched for answers to the most devastating diseases in modern times, only to find that many of them are caused—or at least exacerbated—by stress. I myself have reported on hundreds of stress-reduction techniques—everything from deep breathing to classical music to stress balls purchased in stores. And although I will offer up some more of those ideas below, I can tell you that there is one proven method to fight life-threatening stress: *Avoid it! Run from it.*

A friend of mine once said, "It's much easier to *stay* out of temptation than it is to *get* out." It's the same with stress. Stay away. Think—really think—to yourself, *Is this stress really worth it?* Some stress is necessary and good, of course. Any way you cut it, there is stress involved in being a parent. The rewards of raising

I CAN TELL YOU THAT THERE IS
ONE PROVEN METHOD TO FIGHT
LIFE-THREATENING STRESS:
AVOID IT! RUN FROM IT.

healthy, happy kids are well worth a little stress; that's a trade-off we're willing to make. But not everything that stresses you out is worth the cost. And some good and worthwhile things—even parenting—cause more stress than they have to.

STRESS IN OUR SOCIETY HAS BECOME A FULL-BLOWN ADDICTION.

It seems strange to say it, but stress in our society has become a full-blown addiction. We thrive on it. We use caffeine to enhance it, and we speak of it with reverence and pride like it's some sort of badge of accomplishment. Before I met my wife, I was hosting two television shows (*Entertainment Tonight*, and the NBC show *One on One*), and each year I was releasing two albums and a PBS special, plus performing forty-five live concerts in forty-eight days—for five straight years! I worked seven days a week, slept five hours a night, and no doubt took at least five years off my life. On any given day I was likely to lose the feeling in one or both of my arms, scream at my friends, and medicate myself with alcohol or sleeping pills at night—all because of stress. I would do interviews on morning radio shows, and the hosts would ask, "How do you do it?" I would extol the virtues of hard work—yada yada yada.

The pitiful thing was that a lot of what I was doing was garbage. I didn't really need to do another TV show. Nobody got saved as a result of watching *One on One* with John Tesh. One album a year would have been fine. I could have played those forty-five concerts over a two-year period. I didn't win any awards for getting them done in just months.

The truth is that I was addicted to stress. When I didn't feel it coursing through my veins, I felt unfulfilled, worthless, benign. Stress was a kind of self-medication, just as surely as the alcohol and the sleeping pills.

I have dozens—probably hundreds—of tips for relieving stress. I'm going to share several of them below and elsewhere in this book. But they aren't going to do you any good until you ask yourself a couple of hard questions.

Do I even want to have less stress in my life? I used to *say* I wanted a less stressful life, but I still made choices every day that ramped up the stress, because managing an insane amount of stress made me feel alive, made me feel I was accomplishing something. If I

STRESS WAS A KIND OF SELF MEDICATION.

was honest with myself, I would have had to admit that, no, I didn't really want less stress in my life; at least I didn't want it enough to change my lifestyle or my choices. I wasn't ready to de-stress until after I had experienced a much deeper and all-encompassing change of heart.

So if you answered no to that first question, ask yourself another question or two: *Why do I feel the need to carry so much stress? What am I hiding from or covering up? What hole in my life am I trying to fill with stress?* Those are tough questions. But if you don't deal with them, none of my stress-busting tips are going to do you any good—not for long, anyway.

If you want to be free from stress, you have to learn to say no. You have to pick the events and "yeses" that will yield the greatest reward in your life. Here's an idea: next time you know your response should be no, don't leave room for compromise. When your stressed-out friend asks you to cochair the graduation committee, don't just say, "Let me think about it." Instead, say, "Right now, that's impossible." And shake your head from side to side as you say it. Studies show that when you do that, the person you addressed is much more likely to hear "no."[1]

Even Jesus had to say no to those around him when it was time to be still and listen for the voice of God. Remember what happened after Jesus fed the five thousand? The people were so impressed that they were ready to make him their earthly king—by force if necessary. No doubt it was flattering to be asked. I know I would be very tempted to give in if somebody wanted to make me their king! But that wasn't what Jesus was there to do. So instead of going along, saying yes, taking on one more thing, he "withdrew again to a mountain by himself" (John 6:15).

When the high-pitched whine of our earthly stress jams every signal around us, we not only lose perspective, we lose an opportunity to hear from our heart, from our loved ones, and from God himself. Before you say

> **DID YOU KNOW** *that the blue whale can produce sounds up to 188 decibels? These sounds have been detected as far away as 530 miles. Listening to anything at 85 decibels or higher for longer than 30 minutes starts damaging your hearing permanently. Which means you should probably stay away from blue whales.*

your next "Yes!" ask yourself if you are prepared to add the accompanying stress to your life.

I look at it this way: if the vessel is already full, where are you going to put that golden opportunity for success or for ministry when it finally arrives? You hear it every morning at the coffee shop: "Would you like room for cream?" Yeah, this time I would. Thanks.

Focus on
Your Finances

While we're simplifying and getting more focused (and de-stressing), we'd better get serious about financial focus. Personal finances are a great example of how quickly things can get out of control when we lose focus. But by the same token, refocusing in this area can reap quick and substantial rewards!

Consider these bits of intelligence for your wallet:

→ *Stop clipping coupons from your paper and magazines.*

Coupon clippers often end up spending much more on items they would never buy without a coupon. Why don't staples like milk, eggs, and bread ever have coupons? Because we always need them. There's rarely a coupon for something we actu-

THERE'S RARELY A COUPON FOR SOMETHING WE ACTUALLY NEED.

ally need. That would defeat the purpose of a coupon, which is to lure us into buying something we wouldn't buy otherwise. So don't fall for clever marketers who are eager to introduce you to their products—often overpriced goods—with coupons.

→ *Write it down!*

Always have a shopping list when you go to the market . . . and stick to it! Studies show that you will save money on every trip if you stick to your list—or at least try to stick to 80 percent of your list.[2]

→ *Try an energy audit on your home.*

Many gas and electric companies in the United States provide this audit for free or a small charge. Even hiring an energy auditing pro at a one-time cost of a few hundred dollars can save you thousands of dollars in the long run.

> **DID YOU KNOW** *that research shows mosquitoes are attracted to people who have recently eaten bananas? This is probably because mosquitoes are attracted to lactic acid, and our bodies release lactic acid after eating bananas and other potassium-rich foods.*

→ *Audit your phone bills every three months.*

Make sure that you've really made those calls, plus see areas where you might want to improve. If you have free cell minutes, it might be better to make a call with your cell rather than your landline.

→ *Bank on the fact that you will save at least $100 a year if your bank has free checking accounts.*

Compare different banks in your area and open a free checking account that requires no minimum balance. Then ask for a list of the fees associated with the account so you don't get talked into an account with hidden costs.

→ *Don't buy a new car before calling your insurance agent.*

Compare the cost of insurance for your top car choices. Also, check on the costs of repairing your new car and the likelihood of theft. All of this contributes to your out-of-pocket costs as well as your insurance premiums.

→ *Pay with cash more often.*

This seems like an obvious one, but if you always pay with cash, you won't get into debt. You also will end up saving a whopping 30 to 50 percent more because watching the dollar bills slip from your wallet will stop your spending. Another benefit of paying with cash is that you'll avoid financing fees from credit cards, late fees, and overdraft charges at your bank.

→ *Eat out half as much as you do right now.*

Studies show that the average American family eats in a restaurant four times a week. That's much different from when I was a kid and eating at a restaurant was a huge treat. Today, most families spend more than $5,000 a year in restaurant bills and tips. I'm not saying that you should always eat at home, but just cut back a bit on the eating out if you want to save money. A bonus: You'll also save calories. Studies show that we eat 30 to 50 percent more when we eat out.[3]

→ *When flying, check out the airports that are a little farther away from your home.*

It might be worth another twenty minutes in the car to fly out of an airport where the ticket cost is one-third lower. This really adds up if you're flying the entire family out for an event. Many of the smaller airports also have cheaper and easier-to-access parking.

→ *Freeze your credit cards—literally.*

This is one of my favorite pieces of personal finance advice from the radio show: if you are having trouble with credit card debt, don't cancel your cards. Instead, put them in a bowl filled with water, and place the bowl in the freezer. Whenever you get excited about a new purchase, you will have to wait for the cards to thaw out before you can put them on your card. By that time the urge will likely have passed. No microwaving!

Big Life Question: Do I really need to buy this?

If your the answer is "no" and you don't have a lot of extra income—case closed. You just avoided an unnecessary purchase. If the answer is yes, ask yourself a few more questions:

→ *Can I afford it?*

If you have to go into debt to make the purchase, you *can't* afford it. So forget it.

→ *Do I already have something that'll do just as well?*

An honest assessment of the stuff you already have could make you realize that you have something that'll work fine.

→ *Can I wait until I find a cheaper alternative?*

An overwhelming desire to *have* something—or a *sale* sign—can cloud your good sense. If something is right for you today, it'll be right for you in a few days. So hold off on buying it until you find a cheaper substitute. And here's the bonus: as the hours go by, your need often disappears.

→ *What if I don't buy this now?*

Make a list of what will happen if you don't make the purchase. If it's a question of paying the rent, that's easy. The consequence is eviction—not good. But if you're trying to decide whether to buy another pair of shoes, the consequence may be choosing to eat at home instead of restaurants for a couple of weeks. You may decide that's a good tradeoff, or you may not.

→ *What if I do buy this now?*

If you have the extra cash, you won't go into debt, and you won't regret your purchase—go for it!

Stress Reduction 101:
Take a trip back to the 1950s

At the risk of confirming your fears that I grew up in the olden days, I'd like to give you a piece of advice that I'm trying to live out right now in my own life. I am a baby boomer, which means I was born between 1946 and 1964. In the halcyon days of my youth, our family lived in suburban New York, with only five TV stations on the air (they came on at 6:00 a.m. and signed off at midnight), no Internet or cell phones, and maybe one fast-food restaurant within sixty miles.

I remember going to Tomorrowland at Disneyland and hearing the promise that "Someday we'll all be connected with portable communication devices! Someday there will be satellites in the sky that will beam hundreds of TV stations right into our homes." Wow, how exciting! Most of that excitement was generated by members of the business world who were lured to the party with their own promise of being able to work from anywhere and use technology to shorten their workweek. Oops. The average workweek in North America is now fifty-plus hours, and we are easily reachable 24/7.

Even when we're at the beach or on the wilderness hiking trail, 25 percent of us are using our cell phones, iPods, or other portable communication devices. We are officially sacrificing the moment to technology. We are refusing to pay attention to what is going on right in front of our noses. We are putting technology between us and real life, watching the JumboTron at the stadium instead of the football game happening right in front of us, watching the births of our children on the tiny screens of our digital camcorders instead of experiencing the real thing.

> WE ARE REFUSING TO PAY ATTENTION TO WHAT IS GOING ON RIGHT IN FRONT OF OUR NOSES.

Okay, so why do we overuse technology? Our researchers on the *John Tesh Radio Show* have found dozens of experts who agree that we are afraid to be bored. We try to fill every silence with a log-on or a ring back or a text message. Also, technology is addictve. There's a reason the BlackBerry's nickname is the CrackBerry. Technology is now so involved in our lives, laws have been passed to keep us focused on the road. Theaters have to remind patrons to turn off their cell phones. Personal safety experts warn joggers plugged into MP3 players that they are now prime targets for muggers.

In the olden days, there was something called "watercooler talk" where businesspeople would gather around the watercooler or coffee machine and have a timely conversation. In the past, everyone read the local newspaper and watched the same TV channels. Not anymore. There is nothing wrong with all the amazing choices we have today. But all of the choices drastically lower the chances that you and your coworker will have anything in common to talk about. (And in the spirit of full disclosure, I should admit that as I am writing this, my computer just automatically checked my e-mail.)

Be honest. How many times have *you* e-mailed the person in the cubicle next to you at work instead of just going over to speak? Even as you read this, scientists are studying the hypothesis that a constant connection to information—especially disturbing information (like, the eleven o'clock news right before you go to sleep)—has a profound effect on your levels of cortisol (aka the stress hormone) and causes a rise in blood sugar levels and anxiety. We are connecting ourselves to death.

So what are the solutions? Here are a few:

1. Have at least one day a week when you and your family practice what is now known as a "technology fast." No Internet, TV, text messaging, or e-mail for one day. See how it feels. There are quite a few businesses who have called us on the radio show bragging about their "no e-mail Fridays" when employees must communicate via telephone or personal contact. They say the results are profound.

2. Don't treat e-mail as your preferred method of communication. Communicate face-to-face when you can, by phone if you can't talk face-to-face, and by e-mail if you must (you

might even send a note via snail mail every now and then). When you speak with a friend or business associate via e-mail, you are at the mercy of his or her mood. You could be making a cute little joke in your message, but the recipient might take it as disrespect or anger. Face-to-face communication always garners the best results, followed by a telephone conversation. Ninety percent of communication comes from facial expression and the inflection in your voice.[4]

> NINETY PERCENT OF COMMUNICATION COMES FROM FACIAL EXPRESSION AND THE INFLECTION IN YOUR VOICE.

3. Use the technology at your fingertips to study the 1950s or 1960s. Google "1950s vs. today" or something similar. Do this with your kids if you have them. Take a walk down memory lane, and be reminded that we got along just fine without iPods and text messaging. I know it seems that your cell phone is an absolute necessity, but it's good to remember that things weren't so terribly bad when we actually had to dial phone numbers (or ask the operator to connect us), when what we watched on TV was, well, whatever was on TV, and when students still got in trouble for passing handwritten notes in class!

Are You an
Internet Addict?

Are you an Internet addict? If so, you're not alone. There are a growing number of people out there who can't live without multiple daily visits to cyberspace. In fact, it's so bad that they neglect their appearance, their wives and husbands, their kids, and their jobs.

Dr. Diane Wieland treats patients with computer addictions, and she says the Internet can promote addictive behaviors and pseudo-intimate relationships. That can lead to online infidelity, out-of-control gambling, and other compulsive behaviors. It's serious stuff. And because pretty much everybody has access to the Internet, Dr. Wieland says 5 to 10 percent of Internet users will experience addiction. There's even an organization called the Center for Online Addiction. They say that it's easy to become so engrossed in the Web that hours and hours pass by before we know it.

The experts say anonymity is the biggest reason people get hooked on the Internet. In fact, 83 percent of Web addicts say that's the reason. No one knows who they are, so they can take more risks—visiting chat rooms, gambling, playing violent video games, even bidding on eBay.

Most online addicts deny they have a problem. But Internet addicts may get agitated if kept off the Web, lashing out at those around them. And people who have addictive tendencies in other areas are more susceptible. If you're not sure whether you're

MOST ONLINE ADDICTS DENY
THEY HAVE A PROBLEM.

addicted, there's a test on www.NetAddiction.com. Here are some of the questions from the online test. If you answer "frequently," or "often," or "always" to one or more of these questions, you might have a problem.

1. How often do you stay online longer than you intended?
2. How often do you neglect other things in your life to spend more time online?
3. Do you often form relationships with other users?
4. Do you find yourself snapping at people who bother you while you're online?

Visit www.NetAddiction.com, or check out the book *Caught in the Net* by Kimberly Young to find out more about Internet addiction.

In Praise of
Growing Older

My daughter asked me the other day. "Dad, were you alive in the olden days?"

> *"Youth is a gift of nature, but age is a work of art."*
> —Garson Kanin

I thought for a moment and replied, "Well, I never thought of it that way, but . . . yeah, I guess I was alive in the olden days. But Grandma and Grandpa were the true pioneers of the olden days!" You know, radio broadcasts in the evening and handwritten letters delivered to mailboxes by the postman. As a matter of fact, the olden days were amazing, and the people who lived them had their character shaped by patience, hard work, and love. And they well may be the last generation in history to own the distinction of being *wise*.

I am reminded of this every Mother's Day when our family

joins together in a ritual that my wife started. A few years back, I did what I always do prior to Mother's Day weekend: I asked Connie where she would like to have Mother's Day brunch. In the past she had always selected a favorite family restaurant. But this time Connie had another idea. "I don't want to have brunch. I want to go to nursing homes and hand out flowers to the mothers and visit with them."

"Wow, no brunch?" I exclaimed. "C'mon, let us celebrate all the hard work you do for us . . . all the love and support. I insist. We want to take you out and honor *you*."

"You can honor me by doing what I want to do on Mother's Day."

Case closed.

Now I'm not sure if you've ever visited a nursing home or senior care center, but for the most part it's not party time. I mean, it's wonderful that seventy- to ninety-year-olds have a place where they can have the care and support they need, but I get the feeling that not everyone is thrilled to be there. There are some places, of course, that are literally senior cities with games every night and concerts and amazing gourmet meals. But not all families can afford that luxury. The average senior home is—how shall I put this?—quite basic.

Our trips into the nursing homes and assisted living facilities over the last decade have yielded some great bonding experiences for each of us individually and as a family. Both Gib and Prima have grown servant's hearts on these trips, and I am incredibly proud of my wife and her passion for serving what she calls the "forgotten generation." And me? Well, I started out feeling like I was visiting someone else's grandparents; I almost felt like I was intruding. That is until I realized that a lot of these senior citizens had no one coming to see them, or maybe one visit once a year. Every Mother's Day I am shocked by the number of moms whose only flowers will be the ones brought in by strangers. This truly is the forgotten generation.

> *"Age doesn't matter, unless you're cheese."*
> —BILLIE BURKE

But it's a generation steeped in wisdom. Once I got past a few of the uncomfortable scenes of dementia and other medical challenges, I got over myself and began to spend quality time with what Tom Brokaw calls "The Greatest Generation." The most amazing thing to me about my elders is their highly evolved conversational skills. I've spoken before on the radio show about how we are a nation that has caught hurry sickness. We have become experts at filling any silences using television and other electronic communication. Our most perishable resource is time, but we spend it on things not at all worthy of that time. The elderly have it all over the rest of us when it comes to the currency of time.

Why is it that young children instantly gravitate toward their grandparents? Have you noticed that grandparents never

seem to tire of their grandkids?
Why?

Well, it's simple. Neither little
kids nor grandparents are time-
bound. The kids don't have a
schedule and their grandparents

THE MOST AMAZING THING TO
ME ABOUT MY ELDERS IS
THEIR HIGHLY EVOLVED
CONVERSATIONAL SKILLS.

don't need one. The result is the most beautiful conversation on
earth: a little kid who tells an hour-long run-on story about
absolutely nothing, an elder who wants nothing more than to ask
follow-up questions.

That's what I found on our very first Mother's Day visit—
wonderful human beings who were eager for conversation. At
first I felt as if I needed to go into rehab for my own hurry
sickness. I squirmed. My eyes darted around. I broke a sweat.

Then I looked up, and Gib was
dancing with a hundred-year-old
woman. Prima and Lucy the dog
were over in the corner com-
forting a man in a wheelchair.
Connie grabbed me from behind,
shoved me into a chair, and
introduced me to Sadie.

DID YOU KNOW *that during
the Klondike gold rush in
Alaska, potatoes were so valued
for their vitamin C content that
miners traded gold for potatoes?*

"She's 102 . . . talk to her!"

A hundred and two? How do you get to be 102? And let
me tell you, this woman was sharp. She was articulate and
funny and very good at flirting with me and my twenty-five-
year-old son.

Sadie was most definitely alive in the olden days. Like many ladies in their golden years, she lost her husband a few decades earlier, but as she put it, "There are some okay-looking ones here, but I don't let them eat dinner with us."

It's quite daunting to sit across from someone who is twice your age. I wanted to ask her a million questions at once:

JT: What's the secret to a long life?

Sadie: Be kind and forgive people.

JT: Do you have any special healthy diet and exercise routine?

Sadie: I eat when I'm hungry. I walk, and I go to sleep when I get sleepy.

JT: You said you were married for sixty years. What's the secret to a great marriage?

Sadie: Marry a good one.

Suddenly I felt like she should be the one hosting that Intelligence for Your Life radio show. Eat when you're hungry; walk; go to sleep when you're sleepy; marry a good one; be kind; forgive people.

"You know, Sadie, it sure sounds a lot different than the way I live my life," I said.

"Well, look there, you married a good one, didn't you?"

"Yeah, Sadie, I married a good one," I said with a smile.

"Good, then. Just do the other stuff too."

I felt like I was four. I felt like Luke Skywalker when he got his first few tips from Yoda. I'm not sure I'm ever going to make it all the way to 102, but thanks to Sadie I at least have a better shot at it. And how about her advice? *Be kind and forgive people.* Wow, no wonder most of us don't make it to 100.

MARRY A GOOD ONE.

Sadie's lessons seem pretty obvious. But our world is spinning out of control; even obvious lessons don't seem to cut it anymore. We must also practice. Practice stillness. Practice listening and kindness. Practice reconciliation. Focus. Simplify. The temptation to be unforgiving and mean and sleepless and gluttonous is powerful indeed. We live in a world where overindulgence is revered and where listening is for therapists. And the people who are wisely spending their personal inventory are sequestered away in senior living communities. What a shame. What a waste of a marvelous resource.

Do yourself a favor. On your way home one evening, go to the flower shop and grab a red rose. Take that flower into the nearest senior center and hand it to a little old lady. Sit for a while. Talk. Get her advice. Listen to her story. Maybe you'll dance. And when she tells you her secret to a life well lived, go out and do that.

Can Money
Buy Happiness?

I always used to say, "No, of course money can't buy happiness."
And that's true, for the most part. Studies show that once a person's basic needs are met, people with more money don't tend
to be happier than people with less money.[4] You know from
experience that some uses of your money give you more (and
longer lasting) happiness than other uses of your money. For
example, paying a library fine doesn't give you as much happiness as going to the movies. So let me rephrase the question:
how can you get the most happiness out of the money you have?
I happen to have an answer.

But first, let's go back and look at some facts about money and
happiness. Purchasing a thing you desire actually does boost the
levels of dopamine (aka the happiness hormone) in your body.
On our radio show we have presented many studies to this effect,
including research programs in which people wore electronic
halter monitors that recorded their elevated pulse rates as they
windowshopped. So, for many of us, using money to purchase a
thing yields a high similar to the high a mood-elevating drug

would provide for someone suffering from depression. But the problem is obvious: just as with a prescription drug, the effect does not last.

According to Dr. Peter Whybrow, author of *American Mania: When More Is Not Enough,* even big purchases, such as a new car or even a home you've been dying to get will only boost your happiness for about ninety days at the most. That seems to be the threshold in just about every test—three months. Once the high wears off, you're right back where you started.[5]

What scientists and therapists have found is that money can buy sustained happiness if used in one distinct way: to purchase *experiences*. In other words, instead of buying a new car, plan a trip on which you can make memories. Or even better, instead of planning one big trip, plan several weekend getaways with your family or your significant other. That means even more experiences with your loved ones, and it's the experiences—the memories—that give lasting happiness, not the fanciness of the experiences.

Studies tell us that we are better off throwing a lot of small dinner parties rather than one big blowout.[6] Again, the memories-to-money ratio is higher when you have more small parties. And camping trips always work for our family because we always end up with at least one wall photo of me with a body part that has caught fire.

> **DID YOU KNOW** *that every two thousand frowns creates one wrinkle? So if you want to look younger, you may want to smile more often.*

What about happiness *doesn't* require the use of your bank card? Personal relationships are a huge factor. Hundreds of research studies (many of them on senior citizens) tell us the happiest people are highly social and have stronger ties than people who admit to being unhappy.[7]

Then there's one last thing all of our researchers agree on when it comes to sustainable happiness without money: gratitude. People who are grateful for what they have are more alert, enthusiastic, determined, attentive, and energetic than people who don't count their blessings. It seems almost every therapist who comes on our radio show recommends actually keeping a gratitude journal. I have one myself. I try to make an entry every day. Believe me, it's a powerful tool. And it's simple. You take five minutes each day to write in your journal the things that have lifted you up, or the things you took for granted, or just the fact that your wife held that welcome home kiss for a second and a half longer than usual. Write to me with a few of your own. I'd love to be encouraged by your gratitude.

Okay, here's the take away. To boost your happiness level:

1. Purchase and/or create experiences instead of buying stuff.
2. Spend more time with loved ones.
3. Count your blessings and keep a gratitude journal.

Sound easy? Well, it's certainly not rocket science!

Take Care of
Your Relationships

Now that you've determined what you're really passionate about, now that you've begun to focus and simplify, it's time to turn our attention to specific arenas of life. In this section we'll talk about relationships. Maybe it's time to be less passive and more intentional in the areas of friendship, romance, and family.

Secrets to Making
and Keeping Friends

Where Have All
the Friends Gone?

When it comes to adults, our circle of friends has decreased by a third over the past nineteen years, according to *Health* magazine. And it's not just that we're lacking dinner dates. We also have fewer people to turn to when we're sad, stressed, or otherwise in crisis. And this means we miss the health benefits of having a strong social network—which can do everything from boost your immune system to protect you from heart disease, cancer, depression, and anxiety.

Marla Paul is the author of *The Friendship Crisis: Finding, Making, and Keeping Friends When You're Not a Kid Anymore.* And she says people tend to think of friendship as something you fit in when all the important stuff is done. But friends are *not* a luxury—they're an essential part of a healthy lifestyle. Here are some of her suggestions for making and keeping good friends:[1]

❖ *Talk to strangers.*

You may have a lot in common with the person you see on the train every day—you just don't know it yet. So get to talking.

You may find out that you both love George Strait and Asian cooking, then—*BOOM!*—instant friendship.

→ *Google your old best friend.*
You may have fallen out of touch since graduation, but your former best bud probably still has all the same wonderful qualities that brought you together in your youth. And if they were a good friend then, they might be an even *better* friend now that you're both more mature and grounded.

→ *Do something new.*
Do something you really enjoy so you can meet others who share your passion. Maybe you like the wilderness. If you join a hiking group, you're bound to find potential friends you can bond with. And you'll be seeing the same faces over and over, so your introduction won't be quite as intimidating.

> *"Character is like a tree and reputation like a shadow.*
> *The shadow is what we think of it; the tree is the real thing."*
> —ABRAHAM LINCOLN

Here are more suggestions for making friends, from Roger Horchow, a Tony Award-winning Broadway producer and author of the book *The Art of Friendship: 70 Simple Rules for Making Meaningful Connections*, compliments of the *Bottom Line/Personal* newsletter.

→ *Alter your habits.*

People tend to fall into ruts. This makes it unlikely that we'll meet anyone new. So pick a different coffee shop, a different walking path, or a different evening activity. Take a new class or join a club. Greet every new person you encounter with a friendly "hello" and be open to the possibility of a conversation.

→ *Prepare some conversation starters.*

Before you go to a place where you're likely to meet new people, think of a few all-purpose topics you feel comfortable with. Two great conversation starters are *compliments*, such as admiring an article of clothing a person has on, and *opinions*—give people a chance to share their views and they'll love you. But avoid religion and politics. Something like, "I heard you mention the new James Bond movie. Do you recommend it?" works best.

> **DID YOU KNOW**
> *that 40% of all people who come to a party in your home will snoop in your medicine cabinet? If you catch someone snooping, say something like, "You must need something. May I help you?" Then they can say they were looking for an aspirin or some other item. Then as they follow you to find the item, gently close the door. They'll be too embarrassed to snoop again.*

→ *Don't keep score.*

There's a natural tendency to expect equality in friendships. "I've had you over for dinner twice in the last month and you've never invited me to your place!" Don't get caught up in this—you never know what someone's reason might be. Ultimately, being a friend means enjoying the time you spend together and not expecting payback.

Big Life Question: What do my friends add to my life?

If your answer is along the lines of "Great stories I'll tell my kids one day," "A shoulder to cry on," or even "A good selection of clothes to borrow" (as long as that's not all your friends add to your life!), you're probably on solid ground. But if your friends are just around to borrow money, take your time, or zap your energy with their never-ending problems, then it might be time to learn the word *no*. Real friendships involve give-and-take from both parties. If you're doing all the giving, then it might be time to find new friends. As author Joyce Meyer says, "Real friends are not joy-suckers."

What Does Your Choice
of Friends Say About You?

The type of friend you prefer reveals a lot about your personality. That's according to psychologist Dr. Elayne Kahn, author of *1001 Ways You Reveal Your Personality*. See which one of these rings true for you.[2]

→ *If you have just one close friend,*

you need someone to confide in and trust. You don't trust people very easily, but once you do, you're very loyal. You take friendship very seriously and never take your friends for granted.

→ *If you have friends of your own gender only,*

you enjoy tradition and believe boys should be boys and girls should be girls. You're more comfortable when people are in more traditional roles.

→ *If you have friends of the opposite gender only,*

you enjoy being the center of attention but don't like competing for it.

→ *If your friends are just beer buddies,*

you love to socialize, but you don't like people getting too close. You're very independent and want to stay that way—and you especially don't like to become dependent on one person.

→ *If all your friends are from work,*

you love achieving, working hard, making money, and moving ahead.

> *"God evidently does not intend us all to be rich, or powerful or great, but He does intend us all to be friends."*
> —RALPH WALDO EMERSON

→ *If you have different friends for different occasions—*

for example, you go dancing with one group of friends and play touch football with another—you're well organized but don't like to become too involved in relationships.

Your Life Partner

THE ART OF
ACTIVE LISTENING

I used to make my living interviewing newsmakers, from sitting presidents to downhill racers. Pee-Wee Herman to Gregory Peck. One of my favorite interviews was with anchorman Ted Koppel. Asking Mr. Koppel questions in a live TV interview is a bit like biking with Lance Armstrong. You're working, he's not. Koppel is the consummate interviewer. He is meticulous. He is thorough. He puts you at ease (unless, of course, you're guilty). Koppel is skilled in his craft.

So I had the chance, right there, face-to-face, one-on-one, to ask *the man himself* the secret to his success. I had my question all written out, perfectly phrased and posed with typical anchorman charm.

"Mr. Koppel, you've interviewed some of the most influential people in the world. What's the secret to being a great interviewer?" I waited for his answer. When it came, it took me completely by surprise.

"I listen, John."

"That's it?" I asked in horror.

"Yes, that's it. I listen. I listen more than I talk."

He then proceeded to dissect the basic questioning technique used by the rest of us: Ask a question. Get an answer. Ask another unrelated question. Get another answer. And so on until it's time for the next commercial break. Koppel listens. Then he asks a follow-up question based on what he hears. Not only does he get great answers, but he honors his guest with his rapt attention.

> MOST OF US HAVE FORGOTTEN HOW TO LISTEN TO EACH OTHER.

Mr. Koppel's point was this: most of us, whether we are on television or not, have forgotten how to listen to each other. We have an agenda, and we are not willing to let listening get in the way of it. Without the art of listening, you risk missing key information. It is Mr. Koppel's position that our ears are in danger of becoming a vestigial organ. Use 'em or lose 'em. What's happened to listening? It's been replaced by interrupting.

No one is listening anymore. We have to shout out our next question or check our BlackBerry before anyone gets a chance to finish what they're saying. By the way, I'm pointing a finger at myself more than anybody else. This is a big issue with Connie. For thousands of people, it has become a relationship killer.

Why is this happening? Aside from the fact that we're all caffeinated out of our gourds, we are modeling what's around us. Interrupting has become an art form. You've seen those shows on Fox News or CNN—any of those live news-talk shows—even ESPN *SportsCenter*! Everyone is shouting and interrupting. No one is listening.

As you might imagine, I have interviewed hundreds of therapists and counselors (even divorce attorneys), and most of them agree that the number one predictor for divorce and failed relationships is (nope, not money) poor communication. Either one or both parties stop listening. Even worse, they listen but hear something else. Strike a nerve, did I?

Failure to listen isn't just a bane to marriages. If you can't shut your mouth and listen, it's going to affect every relationship you have—parent-child relationships, dating relationships, work relationships, friendships. Men love to banter back and forth with

PRACTICE *ACTIVE* LISTENING.

their buddies, to shout each other down over who's the greatest running back ever or whether *Animal House* is funnier than *Caddyshack*. Nothing wrong with that. But be sure you can also listen when it's time to listen.

Here's your assignment. Do what the experts in this field say to do. Practice *active* listening. When someone wants your attention—your date, your boss, the principal, your kids, whoever—do this:

→ Invite the other person to sit down. Standing communicates body language messages that you don't want to communicate.

→ Look the person directly in the eye. Don't leave yourself open to any distractions.

→ When the other person finishes, ask a follow-up question (or two) that relates to what they told you.

→ Then, when it's your turn to speak, practice what my therapist friend Mike Smalley calls "drive-through-therapy." You know how it works; you give your order at the drive-through, and the guy with the headset repeats it back to make sure he heard you right. Pretend you're the guy with the headset. When the other person finishes his or her speech (or complaint or tirade), repeat it back—calmly and with love. For example, "What I'm hearing you say is that it makes you crazy when I come home late for dinner without calling. Is that right?" Keep "repeating the order" until you get it right!

Listening. It's an old-school gift that we don't give anymore. But we can all relearn it. Try these tips for active listening and all your relationships will improve. And if you're in the middle of a conversation and you find it tempting to talk instead of listen, picture Ted Koppel's scowl. That should do the trick.

How to Be
a Great Date

I know, I know—a lot of the relationship advice in this section is marriage and family advice. But traditionally the way we get to marriage and family is by dating. (And even if you are married, you still need to be a great date for your spouse.) The "Dating and Relationships" channel on our Web site gets a great deal of attention as our listeners dig deeper to follow up on the stories we share on the air. There are a lot of very intelligent people studying the art of the successful relationship. Here's a lightning round of some of the best information I've been able to learn from the experts who have contributed to our radio show.

→ *Be flexible.*

It's good to have a plan for the date, but the best way to set up plans these days is to offer your date a few choices of what you can do. Say, "After dinner would you rather go listen to some live music or see a movie?" This way you're showing that you don't have to be in control all the time.

→ *Remember to turn off your cell phone.*

Unless you have children or you're waiting for news about a liver transplant, turn the cell phone off. It's too tempting to keep checking who is calling each time it rings, and your date might just think it's another man or woman. Turn it off. The same thing goes for your BlackBerry. It's disrespectful to divide your attention between the person in front of you and a beeping little piece of plastic. It also says, "You're only semi-important to me."

→ *Cool it with the lavish compliments.*

I know someone who went on a first date with a potential suitor who lavished her with praise. He loved everything from her eyes to her long flowing hair to her gorgeous dress. He told her she was the smartest, most beautiful, funniest, sweetest, most caring woman on the planet. The problem is that before the date they only had one conversation—on the phone! So it all seemed extremely phony. How did he know her? He didn't, so his words and compliments seemed superficial and worked against him. It was almost as if he was handing her a line. It's better to say something meaningful, such as, "That's a gorgeous color of yellow on you," or "You're really funny." Just stick to one compliment and mean it.

→ *Be careful behind the wheel.*

This one is especially for the men. Don't act like you're driving the Indy 500. Men are guilty of trying to show off for dates by speeding and weaving in and out of traffic. This actually frightens women. They won't feel safe in your presence. You're just not impressing her with your macho stuff behind the wheel, so cool it. If you do anything that makes your date feel like she's not as safe as she would be at home in her den watching TV, then you're messing up.

→ *It's no longer cool to play it cool.*

No doubt you've heard the "three-day rule"—wait three days after a date to call. Whoever made up that rule was dating at least ten years ago. If you like someone and had a great time, call him or her right away. This shows interest and will most likely result in a follow-up date. You'll also set yourself apart from all the other people who are still following that silly three-day rule.

→ *Chivalry is not dead.*

Men, open doors for your date. Pull her chair out for her. And be on time.

→ *Treat everyone you encounter with respect and kindness.*

This goes for both men and women. How you treat the maître d' or the wait staff or the valet parker is how your date will think you are going to treat him or her one day.

→ *Don't hang out in bars or clubs.*

The best place to find a suitable mate is to follow your own passion. If you love movies, take an extension course on moviemaking at the local college. If you like to dance, take dance lessons at a studio. If you like to help people, volunteer in an area that is important to you. If you surround yourself with like-minded people, you will jump-start your chances of finding The One.

→ *And finally . . . throw away that mental list.*

You know the list I'm talking about—the one that describes your perfect mate. All the experts I've interviewed agree that beyond a few "deal breaker" issues (religious convictions, kids or no kids, etc.), you shouldn't be too set in your ideas of what God might have in mind for you as far as a mate. You need to realize that finding someone who challenges your expectations may be just what you need to come alive. My wife is a crazy, wonderful Italian woman who does not care for action movies, loud progressive rock music, ice cream with whipped cream, or the iPhone. However, she shares my faith, my parenting philosophy, my politics, and my love for family vacations. If I had come into my relationship with Connie with a list, I would have ended up a lonely guy . . . with a list.

> **DID YOU KNOW** *that by simply lifting a spoon full of soup to your mouth you use 30 joints in your wrist, fingers, arm, and shoulder?*

Marriage, Inc.

Once you've found the love of your life, keep your relationship healthy by making time for each other. In 2006, 6 percent of couples who filed for divorce said it was because their spouse was a "workaholic." Having a solid work ethic shouldn't mean you have to sacrifice your home life. In fact, some of those skills you use every day on the job could help *save* your relationship! So start applying your on-the-job abilities at home. The following tips come from Rodale Publishing.[3]

→ *Treat your loved one like a client.*

When an important client has a problem, you probably bend over backward to make them happy, right? So why would you treat your spouse worse than a business associate? Dr. Emily Nagoski, a psychologist at Indiana University, says people lose track of their problem-solving skills once emotions get involved. She says if you act as if *your* point of view is more *right* than your partner's, you'll never find a solution. So the next time you're in an argument at home, take a deep breath and ask yourself, *How would I react if this were a client?*

→ *Be punctual.*

You don't show up late to work because you don't want to get fired. So treat your partner with the same respect. If you make plans for dinner, a movie night, or a walk in the park, don't break your promise!

→ *Set goals.*

Your boss gives you goals at work so he or she has a way to measure your success. So think about your relationship the same way. Just as you have sales quotas or project milestones at work, come up with some goals you and your spouse can work on together. Save for a down payment on a home or work toward a special vacation. Dr. Nagoski says this will create a sense of team-work in your relationship.

→ *Monitor your in-box.*

You know that stack of paperwork on your desk at work? Sure, it's annoying to fill out invoices and to follow up on e-mails, but you do those anyway, because *it's your job!* Relationships require the same kind of maintenance. Nobody really *wants* to do chores, spend holidays with the in-laws, or have those long, drawn-out state of the romance talks, but you should do them anyway. If you don't, your obligations will start to pile up, and so will your partner's resentment. So do the tasks in your relationship in-box to avoid arguments.

Along the same lines, some of the best marriage advice I've ever heard is that you should think of your marital union as a business; it's actually the most important business that you're involved with for the rest of your life. Call it Marriage, Inc.

If you don't put time into your business—say it's a store or a computer company—then you won't sell products, you'll flounder, and you'll go out of business. If you don't put time into your marriage, then it will flounder too, and you will be out of the marriage business. So many people think, *Okay, I'm married now. That's settled. I don't have to put too much work into it.* Not true. Marriage is work, but that doesn't take the romance out of it—not if you're creative.

In any business, the first step is to look to the future. If you don't have any hopeful future plans, things become a bit dismal. It's the same with marriage. So here is a major relationship tip: you should always have something to look forward to in your marriage. Just the other day, Connie and I made plans to go to Disneyland at the end of the month. It's close to our house, and we've gone there many times in the past. It's great even to make small plans for a day driving trip because it gives us something to look forward to as a family. We also schedule family game nights when we invite two other families over and play running charades or board games. It seems goofy, but it becomes great, simple fellowship. It's good for the corporation.

Here are a few other ways to make the business of your marriage work:

→ *Keep track of your financial health.*

Money, after all, is one of the top issues couples fight about. When you consider how many divorces result from fights about money, you don't want to take this lightly. Agree to agree on money matters and (this is extremely important) have full disclosure with your spouse. Being on the same page financially also helps tremendously when you're planning for your future. As in any business, you will talk about expanding. When will you buy a bigger house or renovate the kitchen? When will you go to Europe? Plan for the big things in life like you would do in a company.

→ *Watch for takeover efforts too.*

If you have a woman on the block who is flirting with all the husbands, acknowledge this with your mate and make a plan together for how to deal with her (or not deal with her). Remember, there are others in your corporation, including your children, so keep a united front from the top when it comes to dealing with their issues. Remember that as husband and wife, you are the company presidents. You set the bylaws of the business.

→ *Don't make firing or dissolving your partnership an option.*

Don't jump to thoughts of separation or divorce when things get tricky. In good businesses, like marriages, you don't just declare bankruptcy; you try everything to save the company.

Six Little Things
Every Marriage Needs

As host of a radio show every day with ten researchers on staff, I see a lot of great information come through the door. A lot of it is focused on personal relationships. Sometimes when I see this stuff I have to laugh, because I can't imagine how I would put it into practice. You know, battle plans look perfect until the bullets start flying. But as someone who has been divorced and then married for fifteen and a half years at this writing, I can tell you that it's hard to see the relational landscape until you've been "in it" for a few years.

Relationships are complex because people are complex. But they aren't impossible. Having

> BATTLE PLANS LOOK
> PERFECT UNTIL THE
> BULLETS START FLYING.

been exposed to all the relationship advice I've come across since I've been hosting the *John Tesh Radio Show* (some of it contradictory), two big, overarching themes have emerged—one sort of scary, one very encouraging. First, you have to be intentional; if you put your relationship on autopilot, you're going to crash.

That's the scary one. Here's the encouraging one: little things really do mean a lot. So you have to be proactive—that is, you have to do *things*—to keep your relationships intact. But you don't always have to do *big things*. Routine maintenance really does prevent the big breakdown.

So, after reading through the hundreds of studies and secretly testing some of this intelligence in my own home, I am prepared to give you some of my relationship favorites. Here are six small things that every marriage needs:

→ *A photograph of the two of you.*

Not a family photo . . . no in-laws. Just the two of you. Experts recommend using a picture that is less than five years old. No kids. No wedding photos. Ideally it's a photo of the two of you doing something goofy. Connie knows I love having photos of the two of us all over the house. I especially love the one from last summer that shows us wiping out in the waves together at the beach. I even have that one on my computer screensaver. Every time you see your special photograph, you will be reminded of your commitment to remaining a couple.

→ *An inside joke.*

Without a sense of humor, your relationship will never survive. Your inside joke needs to be something very personal. Perhaps it's a secret word for something or a weird nickname. And—this is important—it should make no sense to anyone but the two of you. Marriage counselors will tell you that when you share something that's just between the two of you, it connects you. I don't think my wife Connie would mind my sharing one of our little inside jokes. People often hear me refer to her as "Ched," but most don't even want to ask. Her real first name is Concetta (pronounced ConCHEDDa), which became Cheddar and then Ched. See, only makes sense to us. I'm known as "Borderline"—as in borderline insane. No kidding.

→ *A fair fight.*

Healthy disagreements should actually be a staple of your relationship. I know it sounds strange, but most experts I have interviewed agree that "no fighting" usually means that there are unresolved issues that will eventually explode. The key to a truly successful fight is to avoid sentences that begin with the word *you*, and never to sling insults. I've caught myself many times breaking the "you" rule, as in "you always . . ." or "you never . . ." That's *never* productive. It's *always* harmful. If your goal is to solve a relationship disagreement, try using *we* instead of *you*. For example, resist the temptation to say "You never help around the house." Say instead, "I think we have a problem with getting all the chores done. Can you help me come up with a plan that we can use?"

> **RANDOM INTELLIGENCE:**
> *If you're telling someone "no," shake your head while you say it. People pay more attention to visual cues than verbal ones.*

→ *A breather when you get home.*

At the end of the day, everybody needs ten to fifteen minutes to decompress. You need to be alone as you shed your work persona and prepare for a much more important relationship. And so does your spouse.

→ *Behaving like you're married.*

What? Yeah, a lot of married people still make choices as if they were single, like putting their friends first or booking a sixty-city concert tour and *then* telling your wife you'll be gone for a few months. (Yes, I actually did that in our second year of marriage.) Realize that from the moment you committed to each other, you became partners. Emotional partners. Business partners.

→ *Saying "I love you" at least once a day.*

I'm not talking the mumbling peck on the cheek—"hello, good-bye, love ya." From now on, look your partner right in the eyes and say it: "I love you." Scientists will tell you that even if you are not feeling very loving at the time, just saying it creates a loving feeling in you by triggering your bonding hormone, oxytocin.

The whole key here is never to assume that your relationship will just fall into place. Just like in your workplace, it's not advisable to just coast through the marriage commitment. You must set goals, have a plan, and show up every day ready to move forward.

Big Life Question: Do I really love my mate?

According to psychologist Dr. Petra Boynton from University College in London, if the answer to the question "Do I really love my mate?" isn't a wholehearted yes, don't panic. Most people will answer, "Yes, but . . ." And it's what follows that "but" that determines whether or not your relationship is solid. If you answer something like "Yes, but I need more space," or "Yes, but I hardly ever see him," you've pinpointed your problem and you can work on fixing it. If, on the other hand, your answer is "Yes, but she's always criticizing me," or "Yes, but he's always looking at other women," you're talking about problems that are not so contained. The two of you probably need to seek help from a counselor to get things sorted out.

And if you answer no? If you're talking about someone you're dating, you might need to move on. If you're talking about your spouse, go straight to a counselor—I recommend calling for an appointment *today*—and get this sorted out!

Happy Family . . . Happy Life

CREATING A
HAPPY FAMILY

What makes a happy family? We have the benefit of thousands of books written by family counselors and medical doctors and PhDs, all studying the family dynamic. And over the last fifty years or so, television has offered plenty of different templates for family life, from *Ozzie and Harriet* to Ozzy Osbourne's family. Here's my take on what it takes to make a happy family:

> **RANDOM INTELLIGENCE:**
> *Kids who eat dinner with their families five or more nights a week are 50% less likely to try alcohol than kids who eat with their families two nights a week or less.*

→ *Routines*

All the experts agree that it's up to the parents to provide a home that's characterized by order and stability. Homes where anything goes aren't really giving children freedom, but promoting chaos. Such an environment actually makes children feel nervous; they don't like living a haphazard life (even if they think they want a little more freedom than they're getting). Children need routine so they can feel calm and reassured.

Connie and I work hard to try to give Prima a day with a schedule, clear rules, and an organized home. In return, she feels relaxed and comfortable, which makes her a happy girl. Her solid home base doesn't waver even when life gives her ups and downs. Of course, you can't always prevent a crisis, but in an organized, stable home, kids know that most of their lives will not change even during the rough times.

One area that's crucial here is having a calm bedtime routine. If you end the day with chaos, it doesn't promote calm sleep and even causes your child to lose sleep. Keep the bedtime routine simple: bath, prayers, a little reading, and a goodnight kiss. Simple. Routine.

"A happy family is but an earlier heaven."
—SIR JOHN BOWRING

→ *Family meetings*

We hold family meetings on a regular basis to discuss anything and everything. My children also have the right to call for a family meeting. This makes for a happier household because family members of all ages know that they will have a certain time to talk about what's bothering them or even to share good news. Children are happy knowing that they will be heard, knowing that they don't have to internalize their problems. Family meetings can also be spirited, joyous occasions. (There is no rule that family meetings have to be about a problem.) This is also a good time to plan for the week ahead and avoid any anxiety about what's on the horizon. How will you handle Wednesday when there's a soccer game for one child plus a swim meet for another child? It can all be worked out at a family meeting, as can vacation plans, spring cleaning, or what to do for Mom's birthday next month.

→ *Family rituals*

We like to create family rituals because they give the family something to count on. This further contributes to a happy, solid home life. Family rituals are also a way not to lose each other in the hustle and bustle of modern life. Connie and I set aside certain times during the week or weekend when all of us will definitely come together as a family—no excuses. It could be going to church on a Sunday morning or having pizza Friday night followed by a big game night. Kids might gripe now and then when the family ritual interferes with going to the mall with a friend, but deep down they love the family together times. Our kids tell us that they look forward to spending time with those they love the most. Prima has also told us how badly she feels for her friends who never do anything with their families.

→ *Play time (together!)*

Parents who play with and joke with their children while sharing their thoughts and feelings end up having children who are friendlier and more generous and loving. Remember to promote loving feelings in your children—not just through words, but through your actions and through your willingness to enjoy your children.

→ A closed door

When it's time to be together, leave the outside world outside your home. This is a tough exercise in this stressful world, but it's important not to always be multitasking as a parent. Put down your cell phone and don't check e-mails while you're supposedly spending quality time with the kids. You can even take this one step further. Try to take a certain amount of time each day and just focus on being a parent. Shut the rest of it out. Don't think about homeowner taxes or the fact that the new water heater is on the fritz or that your contractor is still camped out in the kitchen. During your alone time with your children, try to shut out everything but them. The rest will be waiting for you, so why dilute the time you have as a parent? The kids always know when your focus is elsewhere. Don't be there without really being present.

I've said it before. When it comes to relationships, you have to be intentional. You have to be proactive. Your family is being pulled in a thousand directions at once; it's up to you to make sure things stay together. The good news is that your kids *will* respond to your efforts to make a great family—even if they don't know how to react at first. Stick with it. You have what it takes to be a great family.

Make a Contract
with Your Child

My wife and I got a great idea from our friend and relationship expert Gary Smalley. It is ridiculously simple: draw up a contract with your kids. That's right—the kind of contract you know from the business world. Then live by it. One of the biggest challenges of parenting is drawing that line in the sand and then not having it move on you. We had a written contract with Gib when he was a kid. Now we have one with Prima.

The contract governs the child's responsibilities and behavior as well as those of the parents. It includes everything from grades to sleepovers to homework to dance class to the sassing of parents. If Prima breaks the rules in her contract, there are consequences. If she wants to appeal an infraction, she can call a family meeting. The contract also spells out rewards. If there are no infractions during a prescribed period, she gets a slumber party or a bump in her allowance—you get the picture. Prima, Connie, and I revise the contract together.

Adults sign contracts all the time—from scrawling your name on your driver's license, which indicates you will obey the rules of the road, to endorsing a marriage license, to completing a tax return. Kids can learn about life by having a contract with their own family. And here's a very important point: the contract isn't usually a burden to the child. On the contrary, it gives the child an enormous feeling of power and control. The child doesn't have to guess at family boundaries. It's a lot less painful for the parents too.

> **RANDOM INTELLIGENCE:**
> *Research shows that kids perform better in school when both of their parents attend teacher conferences and PTA meetings.*

The real beauty of the contract, as Smalley taught us, is to have the kids come up with the punishments. The parents provide the child with a menu of possible punishments. No dance class for a day, no cell phone for a week, no sleepovers for a month, and so on. When drawing up the contract, the kid chooses which punishment fits each behavior.

THE REAL BEAUTY OF THE CONTRACT IS TO HAVE THE KIDS COME UP WITH THE PUNISHMENTS.

The amazing thing to us was that, as we were drawing up the contracts, every single time we suggested a punishment for a certain infraction, the kids made the punishment harder. The fact is that kids want to succeed, and they believe they can fulfill the contract. So they have no problem picking the tougher consequences. When you let them choose the punishment, it truly becomes their goal not

to mess up. And here's the big take away from this: the reaction from us as parents is rarely random anymore. There's no
screaming and no threats. Crime and punishment, and we all
move on.

Teens, Sleep,
and Grades

Since the beginning of time (or at least since I was a teenager), parents have been fighting to kick their teens out of bed in the morning. Parents, I have good news: your teenager isn't lazy. He or she really does need more sleep.

RANDOM INTELLIGENCE:
If your teen is a new driver, don't let him or her drive after 10:00 p.m. Studies show that the rate of car accidents involving teens is highest between 10:00 p.m. and midnight.[4]

I have reported on a number of studies that have found that most teens need a little more than nine hours of sleep every night. It's all about their changing hormones. Teenagers are in a critical growth stage, and more hormones are released during slumber time. But with our kids usually going to bed around 11:00 p.m. and having to be up to get ready for school at 7:00 a.m. or earlier, they're not getting anywhere near enough sleep to function the way they should.

Some schools are responding to this problem by creating

later start times. The results have been extraordinary. Grades are up and dropout rates are down. Study results show that students who don't get enough sleep usually get Cs and Ds, while well-rested kids get As and Bs. Teachers also say that delayed start times for school result in livelier classes with more student participation. It's easy to see why; the kids are actually awake!

Why, exactly, are grades up at these late-starting schools? When the body is resting, the brain's neurons still buzz and chatter. Sleep solidifies memories, so the homework your teen does before bed really has time to solidify during the night. Kids who study and then get a good night's sleep usually remember more of what they're learning and do better on exams.

> A LACK OF SLEEP MAKES KIDS CRANKY AND MORE LIKELY TO ACT OUT.

By the way, behavioral problems among kids in middle school and high school significantly disappear when they get more sleep. The reason? A lack of sleep makes kids cranky and more likely to act out. Remember that the teen brain lacks some control over strong emotions, which can lead to mood swings. Sleep helps in this department too.

→ *BONUS tip:*

If your teen is griping that she just can't study for her algebra exam because it's too hard, tell her to put on her athletic shoes and pound the pavement. A ten-minute walk can actually calm the mind and help memory retention for children as well as adults. Exercise spikes your serotonin, epinephrine, norepinephrine, and acetylcholine. These are the exact chemicals that come into use when we need extra brainpower and memory retention. Researchers at East Carolina University found that kids who did ten-minute bursts of activity throughout the day—like jogging or jumping rope—were better at focusing on their schoolwork and following classroom rules! And it especially helped kids who weren't very good at paying attention to begin with.[5]

Kid Wisdom

As TV host Art Linkletter used to say, "Kids say the darndest things." Well, kids can be very wise too. So here are a few big lessons you can learn from your kids, courtesy of the *Men's Health* website:

→ *Asking questions is how you figure things out.*

Ask lots of questions. That's why your favorite question should be the one that tops every kid's list: "Why?" As in, "Why am I upset right now?" "Why do I want to move to Ohio?" "Why am I looking for a big paycheck when I could have a job that fuels my passions?" Challenge yourself to find out your true motivations.

→ *Your body is made to shoot hoops, throw baseballs, and jump off diving boards.*

The word "fitness" doesn't exist in the secret language of kids; they say "having fun." So, make exercise fun! Take up biking, tennis, or skateboarding. When exercise is fun, people are more likely to stick with it.

➔ *There's a reason eight-year-olds get an allowance, not a credit card.*

You're supposed to save up *before* you buy a new toy. Research shows we spend as much as *five times more* when we pay with a credit card instead of cash. So, when you go shopping, buy only what you can buy with cash.

➔ *"I never had friends later like the ones I had when I was twelve,"*

says the character Gordie Lachance in the movie *Stand by Me.* The trick is to try to be the friend you were at that age: fun-loving and loyal, with no strings attached. And people with close friends can live up to ten years longer.

➔ *The coolest adults are the ones who take the time to really listen.*

And you want to grow up to be cool, right? So *listen* to the people around you. And the next time you're with others, try being silent for five full minutes. You'd be surprised what you might learn about someone if you'd only let them talk.

And the final kid tidbit: if there's even the *slightest* doubt, hit the bathroom before you leave! Smarter words were never spoken.

DID YOU KNOW *that a lump of pure gold the size of a matchbox can be flattened into a sheet the size of a tennis court?*

Take Care of Your Health

It's hard to keep the rest of your life together when your body is falling apart. Living intelligently requires that you make choices every day to maintain your physical health. I'm no medical expert, but I do know that a few good habits will go a long way toward ensuring that you feel your best—alert, energetic, strong. There are aspects of your health that you can't control, of course. Intelligent health is all about taking control of what you can control—especially diet, exercise, rest, and stress.

Intelligence for
Your Health

Because I host *Intelligence for Your Life*, people can't help but ask, "Do you actually live this stuff? How has it changed your life?"

Well, one of the topics that always gets my attention is longevity. When you reach a certain age (mine), you start to count the days. I know, it sounds macabre, but I grew up in a Southern-fried household in the 1950s and 1960s, and there wasn't too much information about antioxidants and type-2 diabetes floating around. Stress therapy was a cocktail and a Marlboro after the ride home on the Long Island Railroad.

> *"Our growing softness, our increasing lack of physical fitness, is a menace to our security."*
> —John F. Kennedy

In the decades since, scientists have had an opportunity to study the effects of poor diet and agents like tobacco on the human body. But even with these scientific advancements, Americans find themselves in worse shape than ever before. For the first time in a very long time, the average life expectancy for kids has gone backward—thanks to our addiction to fast food and the resultant epidemic of childhood diabetes.

AMERICANS FIND THEMSELVES IN WORSE SHAPE THAN EVER BEFORE.

I try to beat the odds every day by following some of the most salient pieces of intelligence I've gathered from our radio program. Here's how: I don't skip breakfast.

Hundreds of experts agree: if you skip a good breakfast, you torpedo your chances of working and living at your potential every day. Because you've been sleeping for seven or eight hours, your body—especially your brain—is starved for nutrients. If you skip breakfast, your body detects the lack of calories and, not knowing when food is coming again, goes immediately into starvation mode and starts to store fat reserves.

RANDOM INTELLIGENCE:
Eating breakfast jump-starts your metabolism . . . and if your metabolism is in high gear, you'll eat less throughout the day.

Furthermore, since you have nothing in your stomach, your brain begins to receive desperate "I'm hungry" signals. If you don't get to *good* food soon, you will freak out and hit the donuts or the vending machine. If you have a high-protein and high-fiber breakfast, you not only have more energy and creative juices flowing, you likely won't be hungry again before lunch.

Here's what I eat:

→ *I eat a healthy breakfast.*

A bowl of steel-cut oatmeal with almonds and one big table-spoon of peanut butter (almond butter works too). The peanut butter melts in the hot oatmeal.

→ *I avoid liquid calories.*

All the research I see points to liquid calories as one of the biggest culprits in the childhood obesity epidemic. When I was a kid, a Coke was no more than eight ounces. Today it's twenty-four ounces with free refills. Kids don't have a chance. Can you believe schools are just now starting to remove vending machines from middle schools? The worst part about liquid calories is that they don't register in your stomach as bulk. So you can easily consume eight hundred or more calories a day and still be able to finish all of your meals. We take a strong stand on our radio show against sugary sodas. Sure, it has cost us many advertisers, but it's a position that we absolutely must take.

> **DID YOU KNOW** *that thirteen people are killed each year when vending machines fall on them? Just another reason to bring snacks with you.*

→ *I spend my first health-care dollar on exercise.*

If you are anything like me, you live with best intentions of working out like a maniac. You're going to run every day. You're going to do a hundred sit-ups and push-ups a day. But then reality sets in. A day goes by . . . then two, then three . . . and then you get so far behind on the workout routine that you give it up for a full month.

The fact is that we will exercise only according to our personality. That means if you are a self-starter, a self-motivator, then you will get it done. Me, I need a coach. I've always been coached on sports teams from elementary

ME, I NEED A COACH.

school through college. My piano teacher coached me through Rachmaninov. So, after many failed attempts at a consistent exercise program, I realized that I needed a trainer.

Most people hear the word *trainer* and think *Hollywood*. Don't buy into that. The bottom line is this: a trainer—either at the gym or one who comes to your house—will help you exercise more regularly. Many times I will mention this approach on the radio program and people call me complaining that they can't afford it. Okay, I admit it, a trainer can be expensive. But a trainer isn't as expensive as eating out four times a week. It's a matter of priorities. And if regular exercise keeps you from needing blood pressure medicine or Xanax, a trainer can be a real bargain.

It is my firm belief that if you spend your first health-care dollars on exercise, everything else in your life will improve.

(Don't, however, make the mistake of purchasing expensive exercise equipment.) You won't starve. You'll still be able to go to the movies. Your kids will have milk money. Just make the decision today. Go to your local gym and tell the front desk attendant that you want to hire a trainer. If you guarantee them a monthly dollar amount, you will be able to negotiate a great deal. I pay my trainer monthly, and he shows up at my house Monday through Friday whether I like it or not. Trust me, I hate it at least three days out of the week. But I get it done.

> **DID YOU KNOW** *that if you stop getting thirsty, you actually need to drink more water? That's because when a human body is dehydrated, its thirst mechanism shuts off.*

Here's a simple fact about exercise: if someone (especially your angry trainer) is waiting for you to show up, you are more likely to drag yourself out of bed and get it done. And if you truly can't afford a trainer, agree with a neighbor or friend that you will exercise together—a walk around the block or yoga on the porch. Guilt and codependency are powerful motivators!

→ *I wear a pedometer.*

This is one of those tips that has elicited a huge response on our program. A pedometer (attached to a belt) measures the number of steps a person takes in a day. Two big studies on exercise and fitness found that people who wore pedometers every day ended up walking 40 percent more each day because they were cognizant of the device recording those steps.[1]

→ *I bring my lunch and eat more home-cooked meals.*

This one's really unfair for me even to bring up; my wife cooks almost every night, and most days she makes my lunch. But you should know that each restaurant meal contains at least five hundred more calories than the meals you cook at home or the sandwich you bring to work. To make restaurant (and fast-food) meals tasty and physically appealing, the food preparers brush them with butter and oil and add a lot of salt. If you eat out less often, you will lose weight . . . and you'll have enough money to pay for that trainer!

> **DID YOU KNOW** *that a single chocolate chip provides enough energy to allow a human being to walk 150 feet?*

Anger Danger

Do you know someone who is angry all the time? Is that person you? New research now informs us that anger is a major factor in the aging process. Scientists at Harvard University found that people who can't control their temper are more likely to suffer lung damage, making them short of breath as they get older. And the damage is permanent. People who are angry all the time actually look older than they really are. Want an instant facelift? Start smiling.

> **DID YOU KNOW** *that your skin makes up about 16% of your total body weight? So if you weigh 150 pounds, your skin weighs about 24 pounds.*

Researchers have known for a long time that hostility and anger create a constant flood of stress chemicals in the bloodstream, which can lead to high blood pressure, headaches, indigestion, and skin problems like eczema and acne. An overabundance of stress chemicals can also lead to more serious conditions, such as asthma, depression, heart attack, and stroke.

In one study, nearly seven hundred adults were asked about their anger levels, and for more than eight years the researchers studied how that anger affected their health. At the beginning of the study, lung power was already significantly worse among those who showed high levels of anger and hostility, compared with those who were less angry. The lung capacity of the angry people got steadily worse during the eight years even after researchers took into account other common health risks, such as smoking.[2]

It turns out that anger is not just anger; it's a risk factor for early death.

"He who laughs—lasts."
—NORWEGIAN PROVERB

So how do you escape from anger's death trap? Perhaps the most important way is to cultivate a spirit of forgiveness. I know that goes against our natural inclinations, but it's not impossible. And according to *Reader's Digest*, research shows that letting go of old grudges lowers levels of the stress hormone cortisol. Increased cortisol levels cause memory loss, high blood pressure, and hardening of the arteries. Increased cortisol can also compromise your immune system and throw off your blood sugar, so it's vital to keep cortisol levels under control.[3]

Here are some tips for getting rid of the baggage that's hurting your health:

→ *Write a letter to the person who hurt you.*

But *don't* mail it! List what happened and how you'd like the other person to make amends. For example, "Tom, you stole my idea at work. Please tell the boss that I deserve the credit." When people who lost relatives to terrorist attacks tried this method, they reduced their number of headaches by a third and cut their incidence of back pain and insomnia in half! If it works for something that big, it can work for you too.

→ *Remember, forgiving doesn't mean condoning what happened.*

Even if you were seriously wronged, letting go helps. In a study of cardiac patients with a history of abuse, forgiveness training improved blood flow around the heart.

RANDOM INTELLIGENCE: *Laughter can help relieve aches because it releases endorphins, which are natural painkillers.*

→ *Don't wait for an apology.*

Researchers have found that when volunteers simply *imagine* a face-to-face meeting that ends with "I'm sorry," their stress levels can be cut in half. It's not really about getting the other person to change; it's all about letting go. The bottom line is that we can't change the past, but letting go of old hurts will make for a happier and healthier future.

→ *So much for old grudges.*

Another very important aspect of anger management is

handling anger in the heat of the moment, when you can feel your hackles rising and your blood pressure spiking. Here are some more anti-anger tips from the American Psychological Association's website:

→ *When you feel yourself getting angry,*
take a *mental* step back, take a deep breath, and simply say to yourself, "relax." It sounds goofy, but it's been proven to lower stress levels instantly. When you say the word out loud, it's even more powerful.

→ *Take a close look at what's upsetting you.*
Immediately think about how to change it rather than wasting your energy on being mad about it. You are becoming solution-oriented and not living in the "moment of anger." The moment you start thinking solutions, the anger feeling can no longer occupy your mind.

→ *Become an instant philosopher.*
Consider this: if you are not going to be upset about it in an hour, in a day, or in a week, it's not worth being upset about it now.

→ *If you find it impossible to talk yourself out of being angry,*
walk away from it—literally. And as you walk away, tell yourself, "I'm leaving this behind, and I'm not going to worry about it anymore."

Take Care of
Your Back

Did you know that 80 percent of Americans suffer from back pain at some point in their lives? They do according to a *Woman's Day* magazine article.[4] If you slump, slouch, or hunch through the day, you might wind up a statistic. Whether you're Googling your favorite sports team or sashaying down the street, you can save yourself pain down the road by taking care of your back now. Here's how, courtesy of WebMD:

→ *Forget standing at attention.*
Dr. Arthur White, a back surgeon and author of *The Posture Prescription*, says good posture doesn't mean standing like a soldier at attention; that actually puts pressure on the spine. Instead, stand in a relaxed, balanced manner. Your shoulders should be square and down, your head held high, but your

> **RANDOM INTELLIGENCE:**
> *Exercising can help a bad back. Activities like weight lifting and aerobics strengthen your back muscles, and strong back muscles help prevent injuries.*

muscles shouldn't be tensed. Check your stance throughout the day—when you're waiting for a latte, when you're in the elevator—and adjust as needed. When you reposition yourself, you can even look taller![5]

→ *Feet before fashion.*

Problems like high arches and flat feet can sabotage your posture and lead to an aching back. Women are especially vulnerable; they suffer four times as many foot problems as men. Why? Narrow, ill-fitting high heels are enemy number one! So, ladies, wear those fancy shoes for meetings and parties, but for extensive walking, slip on comfortable shoes with heels no higher than an inch and a half.

→ *Slump less, break more.*

Between work, Web surfing, and TV time, most of us probably spend most of our day sitting. That's murder on our backs! Top it off with bad posture, and we're in for a lifetime of *ouch*. A Swedish study shows that sitting increases the force on your spine by 140 percent compared to when you stand! If you slump, that number goes up to 185 percent! So, here's how to sit:

- Line up your head over your shoulders, shoulders over your hips.
- Rest on your "sitz bones"—those are the two bones in your tush.

- Put your feet flat on the floor, with your legs at a 90-degree angle.
- Also, take breaks every forty-five to sixty minutes to prevent strain.

Yes, it sounds like a lot to remember. But it will keep you from developing back pain that you won't be able to forget!

Three Mistakes That May Be
Hurting Your Heart

We've already talked quite a bit about finding the passions of your heart and pursuing them. But we'd better not forget your real heart—the one that's pumping blood through your body. If your heart isn't working as it should, you're going to have a hard time pursuing your heart's desires! Here are three big mistakes you might be making right now that increase your risk of heart disease:

→ *Mistake #1: Grabbing that salt shaker.*

According to a study in the *British Medical Journal*, lowering your salt intake by just 25 percent reduces your risk of heart disease by almost 30 percent. This study recommends keeping your intake below one teaspoon of table salt a day and avoiding commercially prepared and processed foods.[6] Take a look at the back of those boxes. They are loaded with salt (sodium).

→ *Mistake #2: Never taking a nap.*

Researchers at the Harvard School of Public Health found that midday naps reduced coronary death by 30 percent.

Scientists believe it's because napping may decrease some of the day-to-day stress that wreaks havoc on our hearts.[7]

→ *Mistake #3: Never saying no.*

When you consistently agree to do things you don't want to do, you raise your levels of stress hormones. This not only exhausts your body but can also cause you to gain weight by raising your cortisol levels. Only say yes if the activity "feels" right. And don't ever let your friends or associates guilt you into agreeing to a bunch of stuff that leaves you no time for yourself. How hard is it to say no? Type in "How to Say No" into Amazon.com and see how many books have been written on the topic. We are a guilt-ridden society, and we are killing ourselves by saying yes way too often.

> **RANDOM INTELLIGENCE:**
> *Drinking three cups of black tea a day can cut your risk of having a heart attack by 11%, thanks to the whopping dose of antioxidants it contains.*

Diet. Exercise. Rest. Stress. Manage those four things, and protect that passionate heart of yours!

Five Foods You
Need in Your Diet

Twenty years ago supplements were all the rage. These days there's more research than ever on the healing power of real food versus pills and tablets. If you want the real healing power of nutrition, the best way to get it is from food. Here are a few powerful foods that keep popping up in just about every diet plan:

→ *Cranberries*

If you drink ten ounces of cranberry juice daily, you will reduce your risk of colds, actually warding off colds and the flu. You will also be preventing gum disease and even certain cancers. Cranberries also help your body fight urinary tract infections. Pomegranate juice is also a good antioxidant, and it's delicious mixed with cranberry juice.

→ *Walnuts*

Walnuts are a great way to get in your omega-3s—the fatty acids that help your body reduce inflammation and increase your good cholesterol. Studies show that walnuts even fight off depression while reducing your risk of Parkinson's and Alzheimer's disease.[8]

→ Beans

I can't say enough about this tiny little food that contains magnesium, potassium, foliate, and fiber. A serving of beans each day is even thought to prevent heart disease and colon cancer. Hummus is a nice alternative if you'd like a change.

> **DID YOU KNOW** *that during your lifetime the amount you eat will be approximately equivalent to the weight of six full-grown elephants?*

→ Tomatoes

Pile them on your sandwiches and salads because they're a great antioxidant and they're filled with lycopene, which can cut a woman's risk of breast cancer in half. Tomatoes also lower your blood pressure and fight bad cholesterol. They even help keep your eyesight in good working order as you get older.

→ Lemons

This little yellow miracle fruit is a great way to clean out your fuel-burning liver every day. Start the day with a glass of cold or warm water and squeeze into it a quarter or half of a fresh lemon. This is also a way to start your fat-burning furnace to lose weight.

Big Life Question: Pizza or Chinese tonight?

So you're too tired to cook. Which is a healthier choice for dinner, pizza or Chinese? Pizza's actually a much better choice than Chinese.

Even high-veggie-content Chinese dishes can be loaded with more fat, salt, and calories than a few slices of cheesy pizza. For example, an order of Ginger Chicken and Broccoli from P. F. Chang's has 620 calories and 21 grams of fat. That's almost double the damage from two slices of Domino's hand-tossed cheese pizza. But the best part about the pizza is the tomato sauce. Here's why: Dr. Mehmet Oz, author of *You: The Owner's Manual*, says you should eat ten tablespoons of tomato sauce a week.[9] It's good for you because it's full of lycopene and antioxidants. Raw tomatoes work too, but when they're made into a sauce, the little bit of added fat from olive oil helps your digestive tract absorb all those magical, health-inducing chemicals.

But don't forget, cooking a veggie-rich meal for yourself is almost always a healthier choice than eating out.

GERM PATROL

Quick question: which is cleaner—the average public toilet seat or the average home kitchen countertop? If you chose the countertop, choose again! In a study reported in the *London Daily Mail* on May 14, 2007, 85 percent of public toilets tested were cleaner than in-home food prep areas. In fact, the average kitchen surface contains ten times more bacteria than a toilet seat!

The *London Daily Mail* reported that researchers say it's mostly because people don't wash their hands properly after working with raw meat or using the bath-

> **RANDOM INTELLIGENCE:**
> *Doctors say the shower floor is where you'll find the most bacteria at the gym. So make sure you wear shower sandals.*

room. And unwashed hands are the primary carriers of various germs and pathogens like E. coli and salmonella.

More than ten thousand people took part in another study according to the same *London Daily Mail* article, which focused on basic hygiene principles, including how often people properly washed their hands (thirty seconds with hot water and soap) after using the bathroom. The result? Only one out of four men and one out of two women washed up properly. Then researchers tested for germs around each volunteer's house.

ONLY ONE OUT OF FOUR MEN AND ONE OUT OF TWO WOMEN WASHED UP PROPERLY.

They found enough bacteria to make people ill on such things as light switches, door handles, and the cutting board in the kitchen.

So what's the absolutely germiest place in the kitchen? The tray on a baby high chair! A staggering 60 percent of baby high chair trays were contaminated with coliform bacteria, which comes from fecal matter, raw meat, dirt, or unwashed vegetables. In fact, in every single home tested, the floors were cleaner than the high chair trays. Forty percent of those floors were actually clean enough to serve food on!

DID YOU KNOW *that a small drip from a faucet can waste up to 50 gallons of water a week? That's enough water to run a dishwasher twice on a full cycle! So fix those leaks!*

So what's a homemaker to do? Pull out the hot water and bleach. If you want to protect yourself and your family from dangerous germs, at least once a week use hot water and bleach to clean the kitchen surfaces that come in contact with food.

Beware the
Warehouse Store

Don't you love shopping at those warehouse clubs? If a jar of peanut butter is great, a tub of peanut butter is even better, right? Buying in bulk can definitely save you money. But did you know that shopping for food at the big warehouse clubs can also help you pack on the pounds?

Food psychologist Brian Wansink says that people tend to eat half of the food they bring home within the first week—regardless of how much they bought.[6] Half a tub of peanut butter in a week? Ouch!

> **DID YOU KNOW** that 96% of people put the peanut butter on first when making a peanut butter and jelly sandwich?

Here's how to take advantage of big-box discounts without packing on the pounds:

→ *Out of sight, out of mind!*

Studies show that one in three people binge when snacks like nuts or chips are kept in plain sight. If your cupboard is so jammed that the giant bag of pretzels you want to buy won't fit, don't get it this time around. That way you won't keep it on the counter where it'll constantly be tempting you.[10]

→ *Divide and conquer.*

Divvy up your tub-o'-granola into smaller containers. Studies show that bigger packages prompt people to eat 42 percent more than they would from sensibly-sized packages. Also, use clear plastic containers so you can quickly see what you already have on hand before you go shopping.[11]

> **RANDOM INTELLIGENCE:**
> *If you gave up five bites from every meal, you'd lose a pound a week.*

→ *Work that extra food into planned meals.*

Cookbooks often include ideas for substitutions, so thumb through those recipes! For example, marked-down veggies can be added to homemade soup, and bran flakes can fill in for a muffin mix.

→ *Shop with a friend.*

You can share the great big-box finds, like bundled multiples of peanut butter and pasta, without going overboard. That way you'll still get the discount, but you'll get home with only *half* the amount of food to tempt you.

Big Life Question: Am I really hungry?

If we ate only when we were hungry, we wouldn't be facing an obesity epidemic! That's according to weight-loss expert Judith Verity. She suggests that you ask yourself that question every time you reach for food and rate your hunger on a scale of one to ten. If your hunger level is seven or lower, don't eat. You may be, in fact, thirsty. Drink a tall glass of water. If you're still hungry after your glass of water, eat then.

Are You Fit?
Take the Test!

There are lots of definitions of fitness. We have had many physicians on our radio program to discuss what constitutes a healthy human being, and each had his or her own slightly different definition. For me, one key to coming up with a good definition of fitness or health is to separate fitness from appearance. If you want to know if you're fit, ask, "What can I do?" not "How do I look?"

A report in the *London Observer* on December 10, 2006, introduced a new category of the male and female bodies: TOFI. That stands for "Thin on the Outside, Fat on the Inside." The premise is that even though many people can get themselves razor thin, sometimes the horrible food they consume to get that way produces visceral fat around their vital organs. And so as a

> **RANDOM INTELLIGENCE:**
> *Put fattening foods in hard-to-reach places, such as the top shelf of a cupboard. You'll be less likely to eat junk food if you have to break out a stepstool to get to it.*

TOFI they actually become more of a health risk than a heavy person who eats right and works out just a half hour per day. There are quite a few studies pitting skinny couch potatoes against plus-size gym rats. The couch potatoes look great in their skinny jeans, but they often end up first in line for the statin drugs and blood pressure pills.

TOFI STANDS FOR "THIN ON THE OUTSIDE, FAT ON THE INSIDE."

So for the purposes of this exercise, forget about your appearance. Instead, ask yourself the following questions about what your body is able to *do*:

→ Can I walk a mile in fifteen minutes or less?

→ Can I carry a couple of grocery bags from the supermarket to the car without difficulty?

→ Can I climb one flight of stairs and not be out of breath?

→ Is my blood pressure *below* 130/80? (Some more aggressive doctors—including mine—believe that number should be even lower . . . like 120/80.)

→ Is my resting pulse rate seventy beats per minute or lower?

Add to those five questions what my trainer Doug Larsen calls a "core fitness test." This measures the core strength of your legs, arms, and stomach all at once. Lie facedown, resting on your forearms with your elbows at a ninety-degree angle, and push up onto your toes so your body is stiff like a board. This is called "the plank." Hold that pose for forty-five seconds. If you don't sag, you pass.

If you meet all these criteria, then you meet the minimum in the fitness department. Of course, you should get a cholesterol test to see what's going on inside your arteries; there's no do-it-yourself way of testing that. *If you failed in any one category of this test,* you are officially at a health risk level.

COMMIT TO DOING WHATEVER IT TAKES TO GET BACK IN SHAPE

Please don't wait to see a doctor. And commit to doing whatever it takes to get back in shape.

One last thing: I personally recommend buying a home blood pressure cuff. Besides being an important health factor in itself, blood pressure is an indicator of your general fitness. When your fitness level goes up, your risk factors for hypertension and diabetes go down. We have a blood pressure cuff, and we're pretty passionate about using it—not just on ourselves, but on anybody who comes to our house. We've helped many people discover their blood pressure is too high, and the next day they went to their doctors and were diagnosed with pre-hypertension!

Survive Your Stay
in the Hospital

The hospital is a surprisingly dangerous place. Last year nearly two million people went into the hospital because of one illness and never made it out because of a bug they caught while they were there. The Centers for Disease Control (CDC) is well aware of this frightening statistic. Here are some suggestions from the CDC on how we can protect ourselves in the hospital:

→ *Clean hands are a must.*

The CDC reports about a third of all hospital-acquired infections could be prevented if patients, visitors, and staff were more vigilant about hand washing. So make sure everyone has clean hands, including you. The rule is that all doctors, nurses, and orderlies must wash their hands between each patient. But it doesn't always happen! If you haven't seen a health-care professional wash up before coming near you, don't be shy about asking them to wash their hands. And notice whether your doctors and nurses are wearing gloves when examining you. If not, ask why not. Also, keep a bottle of hand sanitizer next to your bed for visitors. Finally, do not touch your wounds or IV sites without scrubbing up first.

> *"When you suffer an attack of nerves, you're being attacked by the nervous system. What chance has a man got against a system?"*
> —RUSSELL HOBAN

→ *Ask questions—lots of them.*

Sure, doctors, nurses, and other hospital professionals can be a little intimidating when you're lying there in your paper gown. They might even act annoyed that you're asking. Don't worry about that. It's *your* health we're talking about, and it's okay to hold hospital professionals accountable. So ask questions such as, "Why are you about to examine me without wearing gloves?" "Why do I need these lab tests? Explain it to me." "Why are you giving me *this* medication?" Asking questions and getting clarification keeps you informed about your situation. And if you ask your doctors and nurses to repeat out loud what they are doing, they might catch themselves if they are making a mistake.

→ *Pay attention to your medications.*

According to a Harvard Medical Practice study, your best bet for safety when it comes to getting the right meds and dosages is to choose a hospital (if you can) that uses a computerized medical data-entry system. Their research showed that hospitals that employ these systems have 85 percent fewer instances of medication mix-ups than those hospitals that keep track with pen and paper.[12] But no matter what the computer or the attendants say, ask your doctor to give you a complete list of the medications you are taking, including dosages and frequency. Then, when the nurse hands you a pill, you can check it against your list.

Health-care professionals work very hard to get it right and to take care of you the best they can. But a hospital is a stressful, busy, and germ-filled environment, and in spite of their best intentions, doctors and nurses make mistakes. That's why you have to be willing to ask hard questions, even be demanding. As much as hospital professionals care about your health, they can't care as much as you do.

Do You Have What It Takes
to Live to Be 100?

Most people are genetically equipped to live into their mid-eighties, says Dr. Thomas Perls, director of the New England Centenarian Study. But what's the secret of crossing two centuries? Dr. Perls asked the centenarians themselves.

> *"Health is a state of complete physical, mental and social well-being, and not merely the absence of disease or infirmity."*
> —World Health Organization Constitution

Of course eating right, exercising, and not smoking are pretty much a given. But people who reach one hundred typically have three important traits: they're assertive, they're purposeful, and they're resilient.

Being assertive means getting out of the house. As you get older, spend time with friends; be active. Being assertive is the opposite of being passive.

The centenarians also say, "Don't quit your day job" . . . unless you've got a good substitute to fill your time. That falls under "being purposeful." People who work well into their old age—instead of withdrawing into themselves (there's that passivity thing again)—still feel that they're doing something important with their time. Working also keeps

THEY'RE ASSERTIVE, THEY'RE PURPOSEFUL, AND THEY'RE RESILIENT.

the mind sharp and the body active. As one centenarian put it, "You make a trip around the world, then what? You read all the books you want to read, but what do you do after that? A person needs to feel that they're making a difference."

And the third trait shared by people who live to be one hundred is resilience—keeping your spirits up, getting through hard times with a positive attitude, not letting illness or the passing of friends and family drag you down. To be resilient you need to believe that life still has a lot to offer. You need to believe God's promise: "'I know the plans I have for you,' declares the LORD, 'plans to prosper you and not to harm you, plans to give you hope and a future'" (Jer. 29:11).

If you'd like to read real-life stories of people who have lived a century, have a look at *If I Live to Be 100: Lessons from the Centenarians,* by Neenah Ellis. Also, check out Dr. Perls's book, *Living to 100: Lessons in Living to Your Maximum Potential at Any Age.*

Take Care of Business

You spend forty, maybe fifty hours a week at work—more of your waking hours than you spend doing anything else. Work isn't something you want to let happen to you. In this section we'll talk about ways to take control of your work life.

The Ultimate
Demo Tape

I receive at least a dozen e-mails every month from people who are interested in getting a job on our radio program or working at our record company—or any company, for that matter. Most of them go something like this:

> Dear John,
>   I graduated college last year with a degree in communications, and I would like some advice on how to break into the world of broadcasting. Do you have any tips? Thanks, etc.

I am always honored to get these letters, but they also make me sad because I feel like some of the colleges today are leaving out a course: Persistence 101.

I'm here to tell you if you don't at least audit that course, you have very little chance of spilling out of college into a "cool" job. And I'm not just talking about radio and TV, either—I'm talking about the best jobs in any field. I am a firm believer that there are really only two ways to get your foot in the door. One is to know someone very important at the company where you want employment. The other is to be so creative and persistent in your approach that it would be virtually impossible *not* to get hired.

> *"Success can make you go two ways. It can make*
> *you a prima donna, or it can smooth the edges,*
> *take away the insecurities, let the nice things come out."*
> —BARBARA WALTERS

I got my big break while I was still in college. I used that second approach. I had heard that WKIX radio in Raleigh, North Carolina needed a new newsman, and I made the decision that, against all odds, I was going to get the job.

There was one little hurdle: I had no prior experience. Zero.

I had taken a TV-radio course at North Carolina State, and that was it. But for some reason that I can't explain to this day, I believed that job was mine, and I was willing to do anything to get it. I started by creating a résumé and then hand-delivering it to the station. The receptionist was nice enough, but she asked for my demo tape, and I was sunk. Where was I going to get a demo tape? She explained to me that the position they were trying to fill was for an on-the-air news

THERE WAS ONE LITTLE HURDLE: I HAD NO PRIOR EXPERIENCE. ZERO.

reporter and that the news director and general manager would be listening to all the submissions together.

However, she said, they were also auditioning candidates in the production studio. I was welcome to read some news copy. I couldn't believe it. This was my big break. My new friend the receptionist led me down the hall of WKIX radio, past all the teletypes and giant microphones, and into a tiny room with another smaller microphone, some news copy, and a tape recorder on a table. My instructions were to read two or three of the news stories into the microphone in a conversational voice while she recorded the performance.

> I STILL HAVE THAT TAPE, AND WHEN I LISTEN TO IT, I CAN'T BELIEVE THE RECEPTIONIST DIDN'T BURST INTO HYSTERICS.

I followed instructions. I still have that tape, and when I listen to it, I can't believe the receptionist didn't burst into hysterics. Of course, I thought I had done a fine job and left with a spring in my step. When I called WKIX the next morning, my friend informed me that Scott White, the news director, had listened to my audition and informed her that it wasn't what he had in mind. He suggested that I go get some experience in a smaller market.

I was crushed . . . but not defeated.

I went to John Malcolm, my TV-radio professor. After hearing my story, he suggested that I book some time at the campus radio station and, as he put it, "do some wood-shedding." I assumed that meant practice. And so for two weeks, from midnight to 1:00 a.m. every day, I practiced reading the news into a tape recorder. I read the newspaper, magazines, anything I could find. I listened to WKIX day and night and practiced each announcer's inflection. I watched *CBS Evening News* with Walter Cronkite and repeated every correspondent's report out loud as it was delivered. Fred Graham, Morton Dean, Bruce Morton—soon I could do them all. I pretended that Cronkite had "thrown it" to me and I ad-libbed reports "live" from Viet-nam. I was a man possessed.

RANDOM INTELLIGENCE: *If you're having a bad day, smile. Research shows that the act of smiling floods your brain with feel-good chemicals, making you feel more cheerful.*

I rode my bicycle back to WKIX and confidently handed a new demo tape to my friend at the front desk. She smiled and replied, "Boy, you don't give up!" Two days later I called the receptionist, and she informed me that Scott had not yet listened to the tape but that she would get back to me.

I had an idea. I borrowed a portable tape recorder from the campus radio station (WKNC) and went to one of the piano practice rooms in the music wing. Within fifteen minutes, I had recorded what I thought was a terrific new radio news theme.

That night I took the tape back to the campus radio station and began to assemble the ultimate demo tape. It opened with my solo-piano news radio theme, and then, using a different voice, I announced, "And now with the news . . . WKIX anchorman,

John Tesh!" I read news stories. I threw out to other reporters and then changed my voice and accent to create those new characters, men and women. I even threw it "live" to Maurice Ghindi, who was with Secretary of State Henry Kissinger in the Middle East. I imitated both Ghindi's and Kissinger's voices.

I transferred the tape to a reel-to-reel tape recorder and then, using a razor blade, painstakingly edited my new WKIX live news broadcast. I couldn't wait for morning. After my two morning classes, I jumped back on the bike and showed up one more time at the receptionist's desk with my demo tape in hand. Her smile was getting weaker. "Listen, John. Mr. White has not even listened to your last tape. He's been so busy . . ."

"Throw the last tape out," I demanded. "This is the best demo tape he will ever hear in his life. Why don't you listen to it first, and then you can carry it into his office and *you* will have discovered me!" She laughed, took the tape emblazoned with my name and phone number, then pointed me toward the door. As I returned to my dorm, I realized that I had probably crossed over the line of good sense and polite behavior. But I also felt that I had made it clear that I would do whatever it took to get the job done. Perhaps those were qualities the news department would appreciate.

Twenty-four hours later my phone rang. What I heard on the other end sounded like chaos. It soon became clear that

Mr. White, the general manager and the program director were calling me on a conference call. Mr. White told me they had just finished listening to my demo tape for the third time and that they had never heard anything "quite like it." "Come in after noon today," he said. "We'll *find* a place for you."

As it turned out, the place he found ended up being very early mornings on Sunday, playing the religious tapes. But it wasn't long before an afternoon slot opened up and I was reading the 20/20 news live on WKIX (while still going to college).

> *"Nothing is particularly hard if you divide it into small jobs."*
> —HENRY FORD

This first break at WKIX was a strong lesson to me on the power of perseverance. And since those times, I have found that employers (including me, now) value perseverance over an MBA or PhD. After all, remember what the apostle James said, "Consider it a sheer gift, friends, when tests and challenges come at you from all sides. You know that under pressure, your faith-life is forced into the open and shows its true colors" (James 1:2 MSG).

Since those halcyon days of broadcasting, I have met a few other crazy people just like me who have a problem with no as an answer. As a matter of fact, I hired many of them, and they are key leaders of my company.

Big Life Question: How can I find a job I love?

One quick way is to take money out of the decision-making process and ask yourself what you would most like to do if money was no question. Just think about what you would really enjoy doing the most. Once you find your life's true calling, then you can take the steps—classes, entry level jobs, etc.—that will get you to your goal. If your interest might not work its way into a reasonable career, then perhaps you can incorporate it into your leisure time. I have a friend who loves to golf, but it isn't as if he's going to quit his job to become a pro golfer. He decided instead to work for a company that sponsors sporting events, including golf, and he also pursues his passion for golf on weekends.

My #1 Job Interview Tip

Some of my most prized possessions are the wonderful e-mails I have received over the past five years from radio show listeners who tell me how our research has helped them ace their job interviews and get the job. We've given out many great tips on body language, dress code, and even voice inflection. But I am about to give you the key ingredient for acing your next job interview: it's the *thank-you note*!

Research shows that most hiring managers expect a thank-you note after an interview, but fewer than 40 percent of interviewees send one. So here are tips on how you can be a standout interviewee:

➔ *Find out the interviewer's correct title,*

and make sure you know how to spell his or her name. If you misspell the boss's name, you can kiss the opportunity goodbye. And get that thank-you note out within twenty-four hours of your meeting.

➜ *Short note . . . great stationery.*

Write something like "Thank you for your time yesterday. I am eager to play an important role on your team. I hope you will give me the opportunity to be a part of your growing company." Wrap up with a sentence relating back to something the interviewer said or did, something like, "Thanks for the book suggestion; I picked up a copy on the way home." Or, "I checked the Web for those trends you told me about. You're absolutely right—company X had a dismal third quarter." It shows you were listening and you are a follow-up kind of person.

If you were interviewed by a panel of people, then you should send thank-you notes to each one. Make sure they are different and handwritten.

➜ *Don't forget the receptionist.*

If an assistant helped you, send a note to that person as well. And while we're on that topic, make sure you are very polite to the office assistant when you announce your arrival. Managers many times take the advice of assistants and receptionists when making final decisions. Get the person's name, write it down, and use it when you say good-bye following the interview.

➜ *Sending the note.*

Some job experts will tell you to send the thank-you note by mail. I am always impressed when I hear that the interviewee delivered the note to our office in person the next day.

→ *BONUS tip:*

As much as I love getting thank-you notes, I think they are a pain to write. My wife has to hound me until I get mine done. But when I get a handwritten note—especially from a job applicant I just met—it really stands out. It's amazing to me that with so much strong research and so many books written about the job interview, so few people write them. A careerbuilder.com survey found that 15 percent of employers would not hire an applicant who didn't send a thank-you note after an interview.

Good luck on your next job interview. And don't forget the thank-you note!

Stop Procrastinating Today
(Not Tomorrow)

What does the word *procrastination* mean to you? If your answer is somewhere in the neighborhood of "It's my middle name," there's help for you. According to *Health* magazine and Dr. Susan O'Doherty, author of *Getting Unstuck Without Coming Unglued*, here's how to quit dragging your feet and get your tasks done.[1]

For starters, most people procrastinate for one of three reasons:

1. Perfectionism. Your inner critic takes hold of you. You sit down to do something and suddenly you think, *I'm not good enough*—so you put it off.

2. Emotional avoidance. You don't want to deal with the feelings that will surface when, say, you have to clean out your ex's belongings from the closet. So you postpone . . . again.

3. Fear. Fear of failure, fear of success—the fear of what happens next.

But no matter what the reason for your delay, you can get the ball rolling on a project. Here's how:

→ *Take small bites.*

You're not going to clean out the garage. You're going to clean off one shelf.

→ *Do something each day.*

Just twenty minutes a day on a big project is all you need to make a significant dent. And before long, you'll be finished and on to the next one.

→ *Envision the end.*

What will the finished product look like? How will you feel when you're done? Ask yourself these questions often, and you'll start assuming that you'll finish.

→ *Shun the slackers in your life.*

You need to surround yourself with people who don't hinder you. The more often you hear, "You have to get this now," the more likely you are to tie up all the loose ends that you've been avoiding.

"Open my eyes that I may see wonderful things"—Psalm 119:18

Business is about seeing opportunity and reacting to it. That's why we stay constantly connected with cell phones, PDAs, and laptops. We're afraid of missing some opportunity that might present itself. You never know when that CrackBerry is going to buzz with news of the next big deal. You never know when you're going to get that call you've been waiting for, so when the cell phone rings, you ignore the people who are right there in the room with you.

The irony is that while we're scanning the horizon for another opportunity, we've closed our hearts and eyes to amazing possibilities that are put directly in our path. We are reacting to stimuli; we've stopped creating what our heart desires. We miss the forest, the trees, and everything else at the hands of our hurry sickness. We get on that wheel in the hamster cage and just keep spinning. And we keep getting the same results.

WE GET ON THAT WHEEL IN THE HAMSTER CAGE AND JUST KEEP SPINNING.

This became quite clear to me recently as my eyes were

opened by my thirteen-year-old daughter and her passion for dance. As the father of Prima, one of my assignments is to share the responsibility of driving her to and from dance class. It is written in the "Teen Commandments" that Dad—or Mom— "shalt walk the teenager to the door of the dance studio, where thou shalt make no attempt to speak with the teacher or any of the other dancers. Thou shalt turn and walk briskly from the scene lest thou shouldst cause embarrassment."

Well one day, consumed by curiosity, I committed the unpardonable. I snuck back to the dance studio to see what this was all about. What I saw made me feel like Lucy in *The Lion, the Witch and the Wardrobe*. My eyes beheld a world previously hidden to me. I saw mostly thirteen- to fifteen-year-old kids along with some eight- and nine-year-olds working out with an intensity that you would only expect to see in a varsity football practice. The music was a cross between disco and hip-hop, and the instructor was putting them through dance routines that looked like something you would see on Broadway.

What was even more astounding to me was that my daughter and her friends, who were all known to me, were behaving as if they were in boot camp—Yes, sir. No, sir. Standing at attention. No talking. No cell phones. No designer clothing. Any local insect could have flown directly into my mouth. I was, all at once, both stunned and encouraged to see what this guy had accomplished with a bunch of kids who, statistics tell us, would more likely be at the mall or wrapped around a video console.

These kids had found their passion and their discipline. Then instructor Leigh "Lee" Foaad dismissed them to cool down and gather their belongings. He changed the music and began dancing himself. At the time I assumed what I was seeing was hip-hop, but this was something different. At times he seemed to be in slow motion. Then his arms and legs would turn to rubber and his hands and arms would shake with such intensity that he appeared to be illuminated by a strobe light. I

THESE KIDS HAD FOUND THEIR PASSION AND THEIR DISCIPLINE.

couldn't take it anymore. I stepped from my hiding place into the dance studio.

Much to the horror of Prima, I blurted out, "Hey, what you are doing here is amazing. My band and I are playing at House of Blues in San Diego this weekend. Would you like to come perform with us?"

"Well, who are you?" he inquired politely.

"Ah, I'm Prima's dad" (horrible groaning sound from across the room).

"Oh, well, what kind of music is it?"

"Never mind that. You'll be amazing."

"Okay, sounds good, sir."

That next weekend at House of Blues was the beginning of a new chapter in my life as a musician and producer. During the afternoon sound check and rehearsal, I introduced Lee Foaad (Breeze Lee) to the band, and we picked a song we thought might have a good beat for him. Although he had never heard the piece, he began to ad lib to the music. My drummer and bass player watched him and instantly reacted musically to how he was dancing. Our violin player jumped in with a Celtic solo, and Lee became Michael Flatley, Lord of the Dance. And when I quoted a piano piece by Rachmaninov, he got up on his toes and danced like Baryshnikov.

That night I told the story of how Lee and I had met at my daughter's dance studio. I got some knowing nods from dads in the audience, who were also familiar with the teenager commandments. Then it was time for this twenty-three-year-old to go public with the incredible talent I had seen in that tiny studio—before an audience of fifteen hundred, *live*, in concert. From my seat at the grand piano, I could see every face in the audience as Lee took the front of the stage. And there it was: mouths wide open, heads shaking, hands clapping, voices screaming, and after four and a half minutes, a standing ovation.

The following day we were swamped with e-mails on our Web site from people who wanted to know more about Lee and his unique style. As it turns out, Lee's mom, Jonette Swider, started the dance studio years ago with ballet only. And on the days when the girls aren't strobing and locking with Lee, they are *en pointe* in their ballet classes with Miss Jonette.

Lee, Jonette, and I soon became close friends. I took the liberty of showing up in my hiding place in the back of the studio more often. One day it struck me. Wouldn't it be remarkable if the world could see the passion these kids have for this art form? What encouragement it would be to have teenagers see what true joy looks like on the faces of their peers. What a wonderful challenge to write music for dance as a tribute to one of my all-time favorite films, *Fame*.

One year and hundreds of hours of rehearsals later, with Jonette and Lee as choreographers and Lee as principal dancer, seventy of us (including those thirteen-year-old kids) took the stage in Colorado with orchestra, choir, ballet, and hip-hop to tape a PBS special. The show is titled *ALIVE Music and Dance*, and it stands (along with *Red Rocks*) as my most compelling and rewarding experience on stage.

> NONE OF THIS WOULD HAVE HAPPENED IF I'D HAD MY HEAD BURIED IN MY BLACKBERRY.

Here's the take away from this story. None of this would have happened if I'd had my head buried in my BlackBerry, if I hadn't opened my eyes to what was happening around me, if I hadn't followed my daughter's heart into a world that would ultimately change *my* life.

So here is my challenge to you: keep your eyes open and your head up. *Open your eyes that you may see wonderful things.* Open your eyes to the certainty that opportunity and greatness are waiting for you right now. Open your eyes to the guarantee that God will place that opportunity in your path.

The decision to take it from there and to come *ALIVE* . . . is yours!

The Value of
Snap Decisions

Want to know a secret for making a great decision? Do it fast! If you mull over a decision for what seems like forever, you might not make such a good one. The BBC Health News website reports that researchers at the University College in London did a study in which they showed a group people a computer screen that was covered in numerous of identical symbols. One of the symbols was rotated in a different direction, making it look different from all the other symbols on the screen. The volunteers were then asked which side of the screen had the rotated symbol.

The findings were interesting: when the volunteers were only given a fraction of a second to look at the screen, they got the right answer a whopping 95 percent of the time! But when they were given time to analyze and

> **RANDOM INTELLIGENCE:**
> *If you're feeling stressed, try yawning. The act of yawning loosens your facial muscles, which is where you hold a lot of your tension. Even dogs yawn when they're stressed.*

study the screen, they got the right answer only 70 percent of the time. The reason why this happened, experts figured out, is that when you only have seconds to decide, your instincts kick in and your brain quickly helps you pick the right answer. But if you take time thinking it over (and over), you will question yourself and repeatedly re-think yourself. And in many cases, you will actually toss out your best instincts! Many people will change their minds so many times that they will pick an incorrect answer. I'm not saying that we should live in a world of only snap decisions. Of course, there are many times in life when you really need to think about your decisions, such as if you want to get married, have a child, or quit your job.

A snap decision in any of those areas could lead to trouble. But this study found that in many situations, going with your gut and trusting your instincts gets you the right answer.

How to Get a Yes at Work
(or Anywhere Else)

Whether you want a coworker to help you with a project or a salesclerk to give you a refund—or anything in between—there are three steps that will increase your chances of getting a yes, says Kevin Hogan, author of the book *The Psychology of Persuasion*.[2] Here's how he says to do it.

→ *Use the right word:* favor.

Using the word *favor* (as in, "Would you do me a favor?") increases your odds of getting what you want because it shows that you know you're asking someone to make a sacrifice. It also implies that you *appreciate* his or her sacrifice, rather than *expecting* it.

→ *Make it interesting.*

Unusual requests are more likely to be granted than routine ones. For example, in a study done at the University of Pennsylvania, people had more success at collecting thirty-seven cents from strangers than collecting a quarter. Experts say this is because most people's automatic response is to ignore a request they hear all the time—like, "Hey, can you spare a quarter?" If you ask for something out of the ordinary, it piques a person's interest. They think you have a good reason for making such a specific request.

→ *Tell them it's okay to refuse.*

If you say, "I understand if you can't do this," it doubles your chances of getting what you want. By letting the person feel in control, he or she is more inclined to help you out.

→ *Watch the clock.*

Research shows that people are more likely to grant you a favor between 9:00 a.m. and 11:00 a.m. That's when most people feel the most energized, least frazzled, and most agreeable.

Be a Better Boss

Listen up, bosses! Whether you like or dislike your employees, one thing is true: how well you *communicate* with them plays a huge role in the success of your business. Why? Because workers pay close attention to everything you say and *don't* say, how well you listen, and how much concern you show for their well-being. And these things determine how employees feel about you, your company, and their jobs. Here's how to keep the lines of communication open so your workers are happier and more productive, courtesy of *Bottom Line/Personal*:

> **DID YOU KNOW** *that a mother hen turns her egg approximately 50 times in a day? This is so the yolk doesn't stick to the shell.*

→ *Avoid the mistake of talking first and listening second.*

When you have a problem with an employee, the first tendency is to take that person aside, explain how you feel, and give instructions on how to solve the problem. But an employee who is approached that way is likely to feel singled out and may become defensive. Instead, approach your employee with a question that starts a dialogue, like, "How's the job?" "What's going well, and what's not?" This invites the employee to share his or her concerns about the job. It also provides a natural lead-in for your observations and suggestions for improvement.

> **DID YOU KNOW** *that on an average workday, a typist's fingers travel 12.6 miles? Also, if you were to type for eight hours straight—the length of the average workday for most people—you'd burn almost 900 calories.*

➔ *Don't automatically assume you've heard correctly.*

No matter who's talking or who's listening, the message sent isn't necessarily the message received. So, to avoid a misunderstanding, listen carefully as your employee speaks. Then, give a "read-back"—a simple summary of what you think the person has said to you. This helps you improve your listening skills and assures employees that you care about what they have to say.

➔ *Don't do too many things at once.*

Trying to listen to someone while you're checking your e-mail or day planner makes the person you're speaking to feel unimportant. And when people feel like you're not paying attention to what they're saying, they spend four times as long saying it. So make an appointment with an employee who needs to speak with you. You'll get things solved more quickly, and they'll feel as if you've made an extra effort to hear them.

ARE YOU
BURNED OUT?

More workers than ever are experiencing complete burn-out on the job. How can you tell if you're burned out? If you have lost that satisfied feeling at work and don't even revel in your own job accomplishments, there might be a problem. Are your coworkers asking if everything is okay with you? Have they noticed you acting depressed or even moody on the job? Have you been snapping at everyone?

Here's a telltale sign of work burnout: the minute you return from a vacation, the happiness and relaxation you felt are instantly gone, and you can't even manage to come back from lunch on time. Another sign: procrastination is your new middle name.

Dr. Alan Shelton, author of *Transforming Burnout*, studies worker

DID YOU KNOW *that there are two credit cards for every person in the United States? If you want to avoid getting into debt, put the item you want to buy on hold for 24 hours. Chances are, once you've thought about it, you'll realize you didn't want that $100 sweater after all!*

burnout.[3] He notes that you shouldn't feel alone if you're feeling this particular burn. Some three-quarters of all workers are hit with this feeling from time to time. According to Dr. Shelton, vacations, days off, new hours, and outside interests don't always help. Professional work counselors can help, especially if you're a workaholic who is stressed out by a desire for everything to be perfect at all times.

> *"If you have a job without aggravations, you don't have a job."*
> —MALCOLM FORBES

The important thing is to find balance between work and other pursuits. Then work isn't the only focus. Dr. Shelton also suggests the following:

→ *Get a physical*
    to rule out more serious health problems.

→ *Take care of the spiritual side of life.*
    It will give you focus. Meditation and prayer can help with burnout because they take the focus off work. Make relaxation a priority in your life.

→ *Remind yourself that each morning is a new day*
    to appreciate. On the way to work, find two or three things that

make you happy, even if it's just a beautiful forest preserve on the side of the road or watching your kids.

→ *Exercise*
helps beat job burnout.

→ *Sleep*
helps beat job burnout.

→ *Drinking alcohol doesn't help.*
It just numbs the situation and leads to other, more serious problems.

→ *Don't transform work burnout into life burnout.*
Make a list of your priorities in life. Even if you're swamped at work, the list will help you see that other things in your life will be waiting for you when you get through a rough spot at work.

→ *Polish your résumé.*
And finally, if you have tried all of these, it may be time to admit that you're ready to polish up the old résumé and find a new challenge.

If you want more info on "job burnout," just punch those words into our search engine at Tesh.com. You'll find some terrific articles.

Five Questions to Ask Yourself
Before You Quit Your Job

So you've finally come to the conclusion that you have had enough. You hate your job. You have built up the courage you need to stride into the boss's office and quit your gig. Stop. I've been there many times in my career, and I have read at least ten good studies and two books on what experts say you should do first. Before you even think about switching jobs, you need to ask yourself a few questions:

> *"He who labors as he prays lifts his heart to God with his hands."*
> —Saint Bernard of Clairvaux

➤ *Why do I do my job?*

Why are you putting in fifty hours a week? Is it because you love to make money? Is it because your parents worked that hard and that's your only example? Or is it because your job is something that makes you feel great? If your job is fulfilling but the money is not happening right now, be careful. It might not be time to split. Sure, you might be able to make more money at another job, but that doesn't mean that other job will make you happy.

→ *What am I worth?*

Spend a weekend and write a personal bio that includes your accomplishments, responsibilities, and all of your skills. How do you compare to people just like you? What is your standing in the job world? Be very specific. Then go to one of our favorite Web sites, www.salary.com. The Web site has listings of the average salary for just about any profession you can imagine. One of the big mistakes people make is not knowing their professional worth. I remember finding out by accident what a fellow TV reporter was making when I was working in North Carolina. I had been working for half his salary for a year doing the same job. I didn't do my homework. He did. Do the homework!

> I HAD BEEN WORKING FOR HALF HIS SALARY FOR A YEAR DOING THE SAME JOB.

→ *If I quit this job, what will it cost me?*

Will you lose benefits or stock options? How far is your commute? What does that cost in gas every day? What about health benefits? Write it all down. Do a spreadsheet. Share it with your family and friends. I'm not trying to discourage you from quitting; in fact, this analysis might show that quitting is a great idea. Just plug in the numbers.

→ *How connected am I?*

There's a good chance that you already know someone who can help you or hire you. Speaking with someone who already knows your background and your track record is much more effective than a cold call. Write down a list of people you know in professions that are interesting to you. If you are serious, tell them that you are looking hard for a new job and ask if they would keep you in mind or recommend you to a client. Most successful job changes are accomplished through some sort of networking, not through the classifieds.

→ *How big a change am I talking here?*

If you are totally satisfied working in your field and want to use your talents at a bigger (or smaller) company with a bigger salary, then you will likely just have to keep doing your homework, spreading the word, and waiting for your moment. But if your profession is not tied to your passion right now—if you would rather make movies than sell life insurance—that's a different story. If you are looking to

DID YOU KNOW *that the pleats on a chef's hat have a specific meaning? The hat's 100-plus folds represent the number of ways a skilled chef should know how to prepare an egg. I guess poaching, scrambling, and frying merely crack the surface!*

act on that deepest desire that I am always screaming about, you may need to downsize your life and even consider becoming an intern somewhere for a while to get in the door. People do it every day. But it is a big change and not for the faint of heart.

Interviewers are always asking me, "So how did you get up the courage to quit a seven-figure job on *Entertainment Tonight* and follow your dream to be a musician?" It really wasn't that simple. I was already doing thirty concerts a year while I was still on the air, and I knew I could probably make a living (albeit not seven figures!) doing what I loved. So when my wife and I decided I would make the career change, it wasn't as radical as everyone believed. Which brings us back to the question, "how big a change am I talking here?" If you're talking about a huge change that will push you in the direction of your dreams, well, maybe there's no time like the present.

→ *BONUS tip:*

If you are married and/or have kids, I don't advise making the decision to quit your job on your own! I've seen that particular move result in more than one nasty divorce.

OFF-THE-JOB

HAZARDS

In case you need another reason to be cautious before marching into the boss's office and telling him to take this job and shove it, consider this: being out of work is actually hazardous to your health. Studies show that when it comes to your health, being out of work for six months or more is like smoking twenty packs of cigarettes a day, including an increased risk of coronary heart disease, diabetes, and even cancer. Even worse news is that young men who are unemployed are forty times more likely to commit suicide than their peers who have a job. The reason is depression. Statistically speaking, being out of work is actually more dangerous than being a guide on an African safari.[4] Think about that before you quit a job that isn't exactly making you jump for joy each morning.

> **RANDOM INTELLIGENCE:**
> *People who drive when they're tired are responsible for 1,500 deaths and 40,000 injuries each year.*

Another study has shown that the mere act of work is great

for your health—even if it's work that you don't completely enjoy. Just being around colleagues and doing something productive contributes to your mental health, which in turn makes your physical body healthier.

Big Life Question: Is it just me, or is my boss a psycho?

Sure, your boss may be intelligent, witty, and efficient, but he may also be horrible when it comes to management and decision making. That's why two psychologists, Dr. Robert Hare and Dr. Paul Babiak developed a test called the B-Scan 360 to assess an employer's state of mind. Here are a few sample indicators that something is wrong with your boss.

- He comes across as smooth, polished, and charming to clients, but with his staff he's the opposite.
- He turns most conversations into a discussion of himself.
- He puts down others in order to build his own self-esteem, image, and reputation.
- He lies with a straight face to his coworkers, customers, and associates.
- He considers people he has manipulated to be stupid.
- He hates to lose and plays ruthlessly to win.

Any of those describe your boss? If so, you might ask your human resources department to order Hare and Babiak's test. And you might need to start checking out other job options.

Taming Fear

It is not possible to live a passionate life if you live as a slave to your fears. Fear neutralizes success. Fear limits your possibilities. Fear is a waste. If you live there, you will lose your life.

I have read many studies on fear, and the one common thread seems to be that most of us develop our fears based merely on being out of our comfort zone. When we are presented with a different or unusual scenario, our body becomes our enemy. Heart rate, blood pressure, and respiration all go through the roof. We feel threatened, so our body's natural fight-or-flight response kicks in. Then we take action to get everything back to normal. We make serious personal resolutions, many of which aren't healthy: no more public speaking, no more blind dates, no more roller coasters, no more plane trips, no more going outside.

FEAR IS A WASTE.

If we let fear win, we lose. We lose our ability to grow. In a world of possibilities, we see none. For the first thirty-five years of my life, I suffered from stage fright so badly that I would get horrible heart palpitations and have trouble breathing. It was my body's way of telling me something was terribly wrong. (I got the same loss of sensation when I was working insanely stressful hours—the kind of overwork that takes years off your life.) My fear of getting up in front of a crowd was so profound that I would do anything to avoid it.

Now you may ask, "How is it possible that someone who works on network television and who broadcasts to millions of people every night could have stage fright?" It's hard to explain; it's just different. When you are in a television studio, you are relating to a camera, and in most cases, a cameraperson who has been your friend for years. When you make a comment, even when you make a mistake, the only reaction is from the TV crew and/or the director. Once you get accustomed to the little red light, there is no trepidation at all. It's a job, only this one happens to include a teleprompter and some makeup.

> *"First you jump off the cliff and you build wings on the way down."*
>
> —RAY BRADBURY

But speaking to a live audience? For me, it was fish-out-of water time. And that's not all that bad a metaphor—confused, struggling, flapping around wildly while gasping for air. I have no idea why I had such horrible stage fright. I'm sure it had something to do with those piano recitals in my youth or maybe some deep psychological wound inflicted by my parents. In any case, it was bad. Even when I was selling thousands of records, I managed to find an excuse to avoid performing live. I can't tell you how many horrible nightmares I have sweated through that included me losing my place in a song or standing up to speak with nothing coming out.

> DID YOU KNOW *that the poodle haircut had a purpose? It was meant to improve a dog's swimming abilities as a retriever. The little pom-poms of hair were left in place to warm their joints.*

Then I met psychotherapist John Hart. A violin player who had a similar problem recommended Dr. Hart to me. In fact, Dr. Hart specialized in performance anxiety issues. One of the first things he told me was that he would not prescribe a pill to cure my anxiety. He wanted to arm me with a plan rather than offer an easy fix that could have horrible side effects.

Dr. Hart's first tip shocked me. "We must perfect your fear." Huh? Yeah, his first bit of therapy involved re-creating one of my worst fears, feeling it deeply, and then doing it again. Since one of my most vivid dreams was making a mistake while playing a live concert, Dr. Hart had me rehearse doing this. During the therapy I would play halfway through a piece, then hit a wrong note. Dr. Hart would make me provide a detailed description

> "WE MUST PERFECT YOUR FEAR."

of how I felt. Then we did it again. And again. It started to become comical.

Dr. Hart's point in prescribing this exercise was to illustrate that my worst fear was the fear of how I would feel if I made a mistake. If I could accustom myself to knowing the feeling, I would no longer be held hostage by it. It would just be another feeling, like hot or cold, hungry or full. His next step was to have me come to grips with the fact that I would eventually make a mistake, and that it was part of the performance.

Next he gave me tricks to use when I did make a mistake: smiling, shrugging my shoulders, or even making a self-deprecating comment. Above all, Dr. Hart wanted me to have a plan. Part one was to own the feeling. Part two was to accept the inevitability that something would happen. Part three was an action plan.

> "Many people die with the music still in them.
> Why? Too often it's because they are always getting
> ready to live. Before they know it, time runs out."
> —OLIVER WENDELL HOLMES

The true secret that lies within my therapy sessions with Dr. Hart is that you, too, can apply to your fears and everything you do. While you are living your life, things will go differently than you planned. When things go wrong, or just go south, you must embrace that change and take the detour. The alternative will always produce failure. So whether you are starting a conversation with the girl of your dreams, asking your boss for a raise, or making a toast at your best friend's wedding, use this three-step plan:

1. Own the feeling of failure. Stop fearing the unknown. Study all possibilities of failure until they will lose their power over you. If a downhill ski racer never fell during practice runs, his mind would be consumed during the race by the fear of falling.

2. Embrace change. No matter what scenario you build in your mind, what really happens will likely be different. Be prepared for change. Your PowerPoint will crash. Your wedding toast won't be funny. You will hit a wrong note. It won't happen every time. It won't even happen most of the time. But it will happen. Count on it. Embrace it.

3. Prepare for your worst-case scenario. Do you have a backup plan? Study a stand-up comic. Watch a scrambling quarterback. These people don't just stroll into their jobs and hope for the best. They fear nothing because they know the road to success includes being both prepared and resilient. So create your own personal rescue strategy. Rehearse it. Get help from your friends if you have to. Fear has no power over you when you create a protocol to defuse it.

And here's one last tip: if you just can't seem to shake the fear that consumes you, then become someone else for a while. It's the strategy known as "act as if." So if you have done all the preparation and you still feel shaky before that big presentation, act as if you're Dr. Phil, Oprah, or your favorite teacher in high school. Think about that person's body language, speech patterns, and poise. Act confident, and it will be so.

And don't forget to bring your smiling face along for the ride. A smile sends the message to everyone (including you!) that you are in control.

Trust God

There was a time in my life when I seemed to have it all, but I was dying inside. I learned that our efforts, our talents, even our good intentions can only take us so far. At some point, you have to turn things over to God. You have to pray, "I've done all I can do. Now I leave the results to you, God."

Coming Home Again

I've already mentioned a little bit about my spiritual journey, especially my reawakening to things of the spirit when I was well into adulthood. I've been impacted by Promise Keepers, by Rick Warren's *Purpose-Driven Life*, by John Eldredge's *Wild at Heart*—in other words, by many of the same spiritual influences that have impacted millions of Christians around the world. But none of that would have made a bit of difference to me if God hadn't used one woman to bring me back to himself. My story is a great picture of how our relationships shape everything.

> *"Don't try to hold God's hand; let Him hold yours.*
> *Let Him do the holding, and you do the trusting."*
> —Hammer William Webb-Peploe

I'm getting ahead of myself. Let me back up—way back. I was born into the Methodist church. In other words, I didn't really have or make a choice. I just woke up one day, and there I was . . . in church. In fact, I was in church a lot. I attended services on Sunday, of course, but also Saturday and Wednesday evenings. My dad was the minister of Sunday school and my mom was the head of the ladies' auxiliary, so there wasn't much chance that I would be home on Sunday watching football.

During the summer, my church life continued as I got packed off to church camp. Then when I became a teenager, I studied a bunch of scripture and—bingo—I was confirmed. At that point, I figured, I was just shy of being canonized.

> DID YOU KNOW *that belts were once a gauge of social status? In the Middle Ages, the quality of the metal and the jewels used on a belt indicated the wearer's wealth.*

When I graduated high school and left home, I had, in my mind, graduated from church as well. I don't think I set foot inside a house of worship my entire four years at college. It was like that Eagle Scout thing. Get those twenty-three merit badges . . . memorize that Lord's Prayer . . . done. And so I set out on a path in the sixties of "if it feels good, cool." That's not to say that I moved into a hedonistic cult. Let's just say my moral compass was spinning a bit out of control.

I left college as a junior after a "too good to be true" offer in Florida to produce documentaries and anchor the news. The next twelve years were a bit of a blur. Crazy money and six-figure success in 1974 at twenty-one years old. Travel to the most exotic places on earth for CBS News and CBS Sports. A failed marriage. More crazy seven-figure success with *Entertainment Tonight*. And the most deep, bottomless depression a man could feel. I was surrounded by stuff. And none of it—my fancy car, my house, my job—meant anything at all.

And then in April of 1991, while speaking at an IBM function in Palm Springs, California, I walked into the hotel gym and there she was, sitting right there on the exercise bike, pedaling away. I had seen her on television a million times but never in person. I pretended not to see her and went about my workout. It was late, and we were the only two people there. I completed my workout (about eight minutes) and headed toward the door when I heard a voice. "John . . . John Tesh?"

"Connie . . . Connie Sellecca? Wow, I didn't see you there." (Dork gold medal for me.)

To make a long story short, we starting dating, and things got serious. One evening Connie said, "Hey, if you like me, then maybe you'll like this little church I attend."

My heart sank. "Oh no, not this again."

She sensed my comfort level had plummeted, but she went on anyway. "I think you will really like this pastor. He is not really a preacher. He's more like a teacher." She took my hand in hers, and next thing I knew I was John Tesh, churchgoer . . . again.

> *"Prayer does not change God, but changes him who prays."*
> —Soren Kierkegaard

Connie was right. This *was* different. Instead of preaching fire and brimstone, Pastor Louis Lapides illustrated the wisdom in the Bible using clips from *Seinfeld* and John Lennon songs. He taught about integrity and about commitment. And he threw down challenges that you might find in a self-help book, but these were underscored with the ancient scriptures. I was riveted. I was encouraged. I joined the church band and started writing music for them. I attended men's events on leadership and marriage building. I became acquainted with the power of prayer and began studying the empirical evidence from institutions like Duke University on how prayer can lower blood pressure and ameliorate depression. And I was introduced to the most powerful messages in the Bible: love and service. People asked what was different with me.

This was church? Not like I remembered it. But it was a new life and a new direction. It started a chain reaction in my life that caused me to leave *Entertainment Tonight* and to pursue, full-time, that deepest desire of my heart: music. Eventually, that led to our radio show. Instead of getting e-mails at *E.T.* asking for autographs, we got long letters from people telling us how they would use our music and our message on the radio to advance their lives.

I woke up early one morning and realized what had happened: God had given us a ministry. What a humbling experience. This was all ordered by God, but it was orchestrated by that crazy Italian woman who had become my wife. Yeah, I think about it almost every day. Connie knew exactly what she was doing. She knew right where the path was, and she knew that I had stepped off it. She "tricked me" into getting right with God. She used her womanly powers to lure me back to the church. And I owe her my life for that.

> **DID YOU KNOW** *that a single breath from a mature blue whale can inflate up to 2,000 balloons?*

Ladies, be encouraged. Do not be afraid to challenge your man to get right with God.

Men, don't be afraid to take the hand of a powerful woman. It can lead you to riches you never imagined.

Guard Your Heart

"Above all else, guard your heart, for it is the wellspring of life" (Prov. 4:23). At first, this scripture seems pretty self-explanatory, until you start to dig deeper and realize that the "suggestion" from King Solomon was really not that at all. It was a warning, an admonition. Our hearts are the "wellspring of life," and you know what happens when a wellspring is contaminated by impurities: sickness, even death for those who depend on the wellspring for their sustenance. If you don't guard the purity of your heart, you risk *losing* your life. With all the madness that is available to you today—on television, on the newsstand, on billboards, on the Internet—*not* guarding your heart can lead you horribly astray.

I have known this scripture for most of my adult life, but it never came into focus until we had our daughter, Prima. Having a kid in the house—or in your car—suddenly makes you hypersensitive to everything. That guy is driving too fast. Those teenagers are cursing. That magazine in the store is disgusting. And when your new sensitivity alarm starts blaring, you are struck with the realization that somewhere along the way *you* stopped noticing all the inappropriate material in the world. You got used to it.

> *"For as he thinks in his heart, so is he."*
> —PROVERBS 23:7 NKJV

Have you ever driven into work and tuned in to *Fluffy and Zippy and the Morning Zoo* only to realize that all they're doing is being horribly cynical, making fun of helpless people, talking about sex all morning, and going right up to the edge of what the permissive FCC will allow? Have you also noticed that you brought a lot of that same cynicism into your workplace with you? Into your home?

There is a great line from *The Untouchables* movie when Elliot Ness realizes he has lost his pure heart in his quest to "nail" gangster Al Capone. He says, "I have become what I beheld." Distracted by the prize of putting the legendary Capone behind bars, Ness uses tactics that he never would have considered before engaging Capone. He became that which he most despised, because he spent every waking hour (and many sleeping hours) gazing straight at it.

The danger we face by not "guarding our hearts" is that we can become what we behold.

I worked for *Entertainment Tonight* for ten years. It was a great place to work, full of some wonderful people. But every day I was reporting on this act of celebrity selfishness, that act of celebrity rudeness, this celebrity divorce, that celebrity tantrum. And, face it, a lot of our sources were gossips and backstabbers. I got desensitized to a lot of pretty rotten stuff as I worked on that show. After a while, actors were not really people to me, they were stories. When a Hollywood star got busted for whatever reason, all of us in the celebrity media were like a pack of blind dogs in a butcher shop.

> DID YOU KNOW *that of the five senses, the sense of smell is most closely linked to memory? If you want a better memory, try sniffing lavender. Researchers found that the aroma of lavender helps you relax and complete mental tasks faster and more accurately.*

Peoples' personal lives became our currency. And, trust me, when you make a seven-figure salary reporting that stuff, you find a way to justify it.

Don't get me wrong. It's not my intention to play the self-righteous card or to bite the hand that fed me for ten years. I only mean to point out that while I lived in that world I surrendered my heart to it.

I have also learned that sometimes it's not enough just to guard your heart. You must fill it up to make it less vulnerable. Approach it the way you would a good diet plan. Most experts agree that if you let yourself become famished, you will reach for the first thing in front of you. Many times that's the vending machine or the box of donuts in the break room. So the smart diet strategy is to make sure you fill up on enough fiber and protein to stave off the craving for a sugar-and-fat bomb.

You can use a similar strategy with your heart. Fill it with positive influences. My wife is fond of saying, "If you don't stand for something, you'll fall for everything." A famished heart is vulnerable enough to fall victim to the world's most tempting vending machine.

"For where your treasure is, there your heart will be also."
—Matthew 6:21

"Above all else, guard your heart, for it is the wellspring of life." It's your responsibility to protect yourself from those people and things that would be destructive to your heart and prevent you from living an abundant life. When you open your heart to people who are negative and disruptive, you run the risk of becoming what you behold. If you are in close relationship with someone who is easily angered, this person could intimidate, manipulate, and control you through fear. Also, if you associate long enough with someone who rushes to anger quickly, you will eventually begin to imitate his or her destructive behavior.

Think about it. We spend so much of our time worrying about our waistlines, bank accounts, and the lines on our faces.

But how often do we say to ourselves, "I need to protect my heart?" The fact is, our heart is absolutely central to who we are. Do you want to live an "Intelligent Life"? Then above all else, guard your heart.

Give Your Soul
a Workout

Would you like to get your soul in shape? Perhaps the first step is to lighten up. As English author G. K. Chesterton once said, "Angels can fly because they can take themselves lightly." And what works for angels can work for us. If you tend to worry or obsess, if you're a perfectionist, if you're self-absorbed, you need a good dose of levity. All those things are sources of unhappiness. More than that, they shrivel your soul. God made you for joy, not so you could bear the weight of the world. Here are some other exercises that can give your soul a workout:

→ *Pray for someone you hate.*

Hatred is a big fat downer. So close your eyes and think, *May so-and-so find peace and happiness.* You can't hate a person and pray for them at the same time. You'll be doing both of you a favor.

→ *Hang up your troubles.*

Before entering your house at night, walk over to a tree and close your eyes for a moment. If a neighbor asks, "What are you *doing?*" answer, "This is my worry tree. Rather than bring my troubles inside, I hang them here. And when I come out in the morning to collect them, most of them are gone."

→ *Get outside yourself.*

Here's one for all of us who think, *I'm worthless; I can't do it; everything I do comes out wrong; I'm a victim.* What do all those statements have in common? They're all about "me"—and what I'm doing or what's being done to "me." Here's the secret of life: stop thinking about yourself so much. Move your focus outward.

→ *Unwrap the present.*

That is, focus on what's happening now. The past is over. When you're nostalgic, you're dwelling on what you don't have anymore. And if you're too focused on the future, then you want what you don't have. The only way to be truly happy is to relish what you *do* have, what you *can* do, and who you are *right now.*

THE POWER
OF PRAYER

Prayer is the catalyst for the life reaction that will ultimately get you to the life you want to be living. It's the true secret of staying focused on your deepest desire. It's your connection to a life of power and passion.

> *"What I believe about God is the most important thing about me."*
> —A. W. TOZER

Prayer is the most studied of all the spiritual disciplines. Research—scientific research—is ongoing at major universities around the world. Duke University has led the way in many of these studies, and its researchers have found that prayer can have a profound effect on ameliorating depression and lowering blood pressure. Prayer has been shown to lower levels of cortisol (the stress hormone).[1] And prayer's ability to get people to the point of forgiveness can play a major role in reconciliation

and healing of relationships. There have been enough successful studies on the efficacy of prayer in healing illnesses that many
physicians now include prayer during their hospital rounds.

> *"Prayer is not an old woman's idle amusement. Properly
> understood and applied, it is the most potent instrument of action."*
> —MAHATMA GANDHI

Researchers at Virginia Commonwealth University Medical
College of Virginia in Richmond studied 1,902 subjects.
They used twins to ensure more accurate data. They found
that those who were committed to their spiritual lives tended
to have less severe depression and a lower risk of addiction to
cigarettes or alcohol. The study went on to say that the
healthful lifestyles of the spiritually rich and faithful clearly
contribute to their well-being. They tend not to smoke or
drink to excess. Their marriages are more stable and their
spiritual communities form a network that can catch and
support them when they are ill.[2]

So what is my own personal experience with the power of
prayer? I grew up with the Lord's Prayer. It was the first prayer
we memorized in church and the prayer we recited at bedtime.
It never really meant much to me. But as I grew out of the "pray
because I told you to" phase of my life, I began to explore a
more informal relationship with God that removed all the thees

and thous and replaced them with a more natural, one-on-one conversation.

> *"Ask, and it will be given to you; seek, and you will find; knock,*
> *and it will be opened to you. For everyone who asks receives, and*
> *he who seeks finds, and to him who knocks it shall be opened."*
> —Matthew 7:7–8 nasb

Talking to God can be a little awkward at first, but if you stick with it, you start to realize that you have a lot on your mind. When you pray with your heart and not your head, you finally get to that stuff that you would never share with your shrink. I recommend praying out loud. And if you want to supercharge the prayer, pray with someone else.

Why do people swear that prayer improves their lives and their businesses? Again, I'm no expert, but I believe it's because God wants nothing more *from* us and *for* us than *love*. If we pray without ceasing, read God's Word, and stay connected with him all throughout the day, then we can't help but behave lovingly. And when we behave lovingly, people want to hang out with us. Our spouses feel safe with us because we stand on the truth, so our relationship improves. Our business partners want a piece of the joy that seems to follow us everywhere, so business improves. We get that promotion. Then the Holy Spirit works with our conscience and plants an itch in us that can only be scratched when we serve others and find our *purpose*.

Listen, I've tried this both ways. Let me save you some time. If you want to live an intelligent life, if you want to have the life for which God made you, if you want abundance in your life, you have to support everything you do with a consistent prayer life. Don't worry about infringing on God's time or asking for the wrong thing. Just have a conversation and be honest.

Just How Spiritual
Are We?

It seems that 72 percent of Americans say their lives have meaning and purpose because of faith. But there's a gap between what we believe and how we act.

That's the finding of a new Gallup poll that was conducted with the University of Pennsylvania's Center for Research on Religion and Urban Civil Society. It examined "The Spiritual State of the Union."[3] To do this, it looked at Inner Commitment—people's connection with God or a higher power—and Outer Commitment—how they live out their commitment through service to society.

Nearly 80 percent of people agreed with the statement "the overall health of the nation depends a great deal on the spiritual health of the nation." And almost as many people agreed that "life has meaning and purpose because of faith." Sixty percent agreed with the idea that all people, regardless of race, creed, or wealth, are connected by a higher power, and therefore we should accept everybody.

> *"I would rather walk with God in the dark than go alone in the light."*
> —MARY GARDINER BRAINARD

More than a third of Americans prefer to think of themselves as spiritual rather than religious. And they defined spirituality in several ways, including belief in God or a higher power, or just seeking to be a good person and reach their full human potential.

But here's the problem: only 44 percent agreed with the statement "I'm involved and try to help the lives of the poor and suffering." Could it be that we're not putting our money where our mouths are? Something to think about.

Hard Work, Risk,
and Prayer

Hard Work, Risk, and Prayer was the original working title of this book before we changed it to match the radio show. But as I have written this book, the "big three," as I often call them— hard work, risk, and prayer—have been constantly on my mind. They are the recipe for getting everything you want in life. It is my firm belief that when we fail to live the life we want, it's because we miss one or more of these key elements:

→ *Hard work*

Are you really up to the task? Sometimes we think we're ready for the challenge, but we aren't totally committed to putting in the hard work.

→ *Risk*

It is much easier to survive in your comfort zone and react to outside stimuli. To embrace change is to risk everything. My antonym for *risk* is *fear*. And if you are fearful, you will never risk anything.

→ *Prayer*

Ask God to get involved. I have "succeeded" at a lot of pretty meaningless things without asking God to get involved, but I have never reached an important goal in my life—a truly significant goal—without supporting it with prayer. And I am not talking about cute, polite conversation with God. I mean crying out like the psalmist and getting God's full attention.

The "big three" have been in my playbook since the biggest event of my professional career, *Live at Red Rocks.*

By now I've made it clear that one of my greatest passions is playing grand piano. Even when I was six years old, I would dream of sitting on stage with a symphony orchestra and playing music I had composed. It was a dream so powerful that it would often jolt me out of a deep sleep. Having been on television for most of my professional life, I knew that if I was going to be taken seriously as a musician, I

> IT WAS A DREAM SO POWERFUL THAT IT WOULD OFTEN JOLT ME OUT OF A DEEP SLEEP.

needed to make a statement so big that it would eclipse any image anyone had of me reading the celebrity birthdays on *E.T.* It would have to be an event so large in scope that it could virtually redefine and re-brand me as a performer.

After much research on the success of other "unknown" music acts, I was drawn to the power of PBS. When PBS presented the special *The Three Tenors,* Plácido Domingo, José Carreras, and Luciano Pavarotti performed live at the ancient

Baths of Caracalla in Rome. It was riveting TV, and it started a new trend at PBS of the high-concept production.

That same year, a friend of mine, who knew I was looking for a unique concert venue somewhere in the world, handed me a copy of U2's *Under a Blood Red Sky*. The band was performing at this amazing place called Red Rocks. It was magical— twelve thousand screaming fans standing between two giant mountains of rock. The band performed under a full moon with a ghostly mist of fog above the natural stage. The venue's nickname was "God's Amphitheatre." It was a revelation; I remember it like it was yesterday. *This is the place*, I thought. *Red Rocks. John Tesh: Live at Red Rocks with Symphony Orchestra.*

THE BAND WAS PERFORMING AT THIS AMAZING PLACE CALLED RED ROCKS.

When I tracked down the decision makers at Public Television, I was met with skepticism at first, and not surprisingly. They were intrigued by the fact that twenty-three million viewers a night were aware of John Tesh. But John Tesh the pianist? Not so much. In short, I got a big fat thanks, but no thanks.

But after a few weeks of my annoying phone calls, they at least agreed to a test. This meant that once the special was recorded and edited, they would air it in a small market and see if there was any reaction from PBS viewers. They made it clear, however, that since I was not a proven artist and had sold only a few thousand records, they could not invest money in the project. And so I began to pray.

I prayed for guidance and for strength. I prayed for vision and for wisdom. I had faith. It was time for works.

After two weeks of financial spreadsheets and phone calls to production companies, it became clear that in order to take the stage at Red Rocks with a symphony orchestra and record the concert with ten cameras, my wife and I would have to borrow money against our home. We had no guarantee that we would get our money back. It was a huge risk, but it was one we embraced together.

> *"Consider it pure joy, my brothers, whenever you face trials of many kinds, because you know that the testing of your faith develops perseverance. Perseverance must finish its work so that you may be mature and complete, not lacking anything."*
> —James 1:2–4

For the next eight months, I worked night and day writing new music. I reported for duty at *Entertainment Tonight* in the early morning. Then, following the taping, I rushed into the recording studio to create new material and arrangements. In the middle of this madness, Connie was pregnant with our daughter Prima. Looking back now, I realize that it was a ridiculous time to try to mount such an undertaking. But my wife was right there by my side, and her strength kept me focused.

On August 12, 1994—with Connie and two-and-a-half-month-old Prima in the audience of twelve thousand—I took the stage at Red Rocks Amphitheater with my band and the eighty-piece Colorado Symphony Orchestra. From the very first down-beat, I was energized like never before. The audience caught the joy from the stage and roared their approval after every song.

Then, four songs into the program, the temperature suddenly dropped, and in moments we were in the middle of a driving rainstorm. Over my right shoulder I heard a commotion and turned to see the orchestra rushing offstage. The rain would have destroyed their delicate violins and cellos. My heart sank. So this was it. We risked it all and got three songs. I had borrowed against the house. I had put my family's security at risk. What a disaster. I watched as the water slammed into my grand piano. And then I turned my gaze to the audience and was startled by what I saw. No one was leaving. They all started putting on rain parkas and opening umbrellas. No one moved. I turned to the stage manager, who had opened an umbrella for me. He gave an encouraging smile. "Hey, it's Red Rocks," he said. "It always rains here. They're used to it!"

Terrific. But how was I supposed to record a concert without the symphony? My violinist Charlie Bisharat had the answer. "C'mon, let's go. Let's play in the rain. This will be cool." What followed was an experience I don't suppose I'll ever have again. I turned to address the audience, "Well, the symphony had to leave, but you obviously aren't going anywhere. If you don't mind, we'd like to play for you . . . in the rain."

The crowd, sensing that they could save the day, roared back at us, pumping their umbrellas in the air. And so five of us—piano, electric violin (I know, he's crazy), bass, percussion, and guitar, with rain drops ricocheting off our instruments, played like men possessed. Charlie was running from one side of the stage to the other, skidding on the slippery rock surface. I looked back at our drummer, Dave Hooper. Water was pouring out of his bass drum. There was a river running down the center aisle of the audience. A cameraman fell as he tried to follow Charlie.

THERE WAS A RIVER RUNNING DOWN THE CENTER AISLE OF THE AUDIENCE.

I just kept praying, "God, stay in this. If this is your plan for us, then please just make sure it all gets on tape." And then it happened. And if I didn't have it on tape, you would never believe me. Fifteen minutes after the rainstorm began, it stopped. And I mean it was like someone hitting an off switch. The rain stopped, the orchestra returned to the stage, and as the audience retracted their umbrellas, they were greeted by a full moon overhead. By this time most of us onstage were in tears. We had witnessed what can only be described as an intervention. We finished the concert basking in the unspoken connection between the audience and us. All of us—audience and performers alike—knew that we had been part of something supernatural.

Six months later, *Live at Red Rocks with the Colorado Symphony* went on to become one of PBS's all-time biggest fund-raising concerts. The album went to number one on the instrumental charts. And guess what the most popular segment was? Yep. The band playing three songs in the rain. To this day, we receive letters from viewers who talk about that segment as a life-metaphor for the rewards of perseverance.

And it was all due to hard work, risk, and prayer. I've spent five years of my life now talking to millions of radio listeners about the importance of rejecting passivity, taking control of those things you can control, and using good information to make better decisions and create a better life for yourself. That's what "intelligence for your life" means. But that's not all it means.

In the end, true intelligence means coming to the end of yourself and letting God take you the rest of the way. I mean *really* coming to the end of yourself—doing everything you can to grab hold of the life you want, not just passively saying, "Well, I guess God has everything under control, so I'll be heading on back to the sofa." No, I'm talking about giving your best in the confidence that God will honor that and give the best right back to you. That's what makes it possible for you to take risks. And prayer? That's just putting into words the life that you're already living: "There, God, I've given my all . . . but even my all isn't enough without your grace and mercy. Would you fill in the gaps?"

Hard work. Risk. Prayer. That's the essence of "Intelligence for Your Life." Are you ready to live that way?

Notes

Introduction

1. Rick Warren, *Purpose-Driven Life* (Grand Rapids: Zondervan, 2002).

Section One: Find Your Passion

1. John Eldredge, *Wild at Heart* (Nashville: Nelson, 2006).
2. Robert B. Cialdini, *Influence: The New Psychology of Modern Persuasion* (New York: Quill, 1984), 16–18.
3. John Eldredge, *Wild at Heart* (Nashville: Nelson, 2006).
4. Peggy A. Thoits and Lyndi N. Hewitt, "Volunteer Work and Well-Being," *Journal of Health and Social Behavior* 42, no. 2 (June 2001): 115–31. More information can be found at http://www.thirdage.com/healthgate/files/78992.html.
5. Paul Arnstein, "From Chronic Pain Patient to Peer: Benefits and Risks of Volunteering," *Pain Management Nursing* 3, no. 3: 94–103.

Section Two: Focus and Simplify

1. Jeff Grabmeier, "Nodding or Shaking Your Head May Even Influence Your Own Thoughts Study Finds," July 3, 2003, Ohio State University, http://researchnews.osu.edu/archive/headmvmt.htm.
2. Spencer Ray, "5 Ways to Save More Money Each Month," http://EzineArticles.com/?expert=Spencer_Ray.
   Cheryl Russell, "Top Ten U.S. Spending Trends," *Business Trends*, February 17, 2006, http://www.smallbiztrends.com/2006/02/top-ten-us-spending-trends.html.
3. One study at UCLA indicated that up to 93 percent of communication effectiveness is determined by nonverbal cues. Another study indicated that the impact of a performance was determined 7 percent by the words used, 38 percent by voice quality, and 55 percent by the nonverbal communication.
4. Eric Quinones, "Link Between Income and Happiness Is Mainly an Illusion," Princeton University, June 29, 2006, http://www.princeton.edu/main/news/archive/S15/15/09S18/index.xml?section=topstories.
5. Peter Whybrow, *American Mania: When More is Not Enough* (New York: W.W. Norton, 2006).

6. Marcela Kogan, "Where Happiness Lies," *Monitor on Psychology* 32 (January 1, 2001), www.apa.org/monitor/jan01/positivepsych.html.
7. Sonja Lyubomirsky et al., "The Benefits of Frequent Positive Affect: Does Happiness Lead to Success?" *Psychological Bulletin* 131, no. 6, http://whyfiles.org/shorties/193success_happy/.

Section Three: Take Care of Your Relationships
1. Marla Paul, *The Friendship Crisis: Finding, Making, and Keeping Friends When You're Not a Kid Anymore* (Emmaus, PA: Rodale Press, 2005), quoted in Denene Millner, "Friend Therapy," *Health Magazine*, April 2007.
2. Elayne Kahn, *1001 Ways You Reveal Your Personality* (New York: Signet, a division of Penguin Books, 1986).
3. Emily Nagoski as quoted in "The Home Office," *BestLife Magazine*, 18 August 2007.
4. "Age, Gender Major Factors in Severity of Auto Accident Injuries," Purdue University, January 2, 2007, http://news.uns.purdue.edu/ UNS/html4ever/2007/070102ManneringGender.html.
5. Matt Mahar, "ECU Study Shows Active Kids Focus Better in School," *East Carolina University News Bureau*, 2 February 2007.

Section Four: Take Care of Your Health
1. Michelle L. Brandt, "Pedometers Help People Count Steps to Get Healthy," Stanford News Service, November 28, 2007, http://news-service.stanford.edu/news/2007/november28/ med-pedometer-112807.html.
2. American Psychological Association, "Harboring Hostility May Be Linked to Unhealthy Lungs," *Science Daily*, June 4, 2007, http://www.sciencedaily.com/releases/2007/06/070603215232.htm.
3. Lisa Collier Cool, "The Power of Forgiving," *Readers Digest*, May 2004.
4. "Causes and Prevention of Back Pain and Injuries," *Medical News Today*, April 28, 2006, http://www.medicalnewstoday.com/articles/42385.php.
5. Arthur White and Kate Kelly, *The Posture Prescription* (New York: Three Rivers Press, a division of Random House, 2003).
6. Marcus Mulner and David Batty, "Salt, Diet and Health," *British Medical Journal* 318 (1999): 471.
7. Andraniki Naska et al., "Siesta in Healthy Adults and Coronary Mortality in the General Population," *Archives of Internal Medicine* 167 (2007): 296–301.
8. Miranda Hitti, "Do Some Foods Battle Depression?" *Fox News*, February 11, 2005, http://www.foxnews.com/story/0,2933,147126,00.html.
9. Mehmet Oz, *You! The Owner's Manual* (New York: HarperCollins, 2005). For more information on this subject go to Brian Wansink's website: http://mindlesseating.org/

10. Mary Ellen Strote, "Six Reasons You Overeat—Binge-Beating Strategies," *Shape*, April 2004, FindArticles.com, http://findarticles.com/p/articles/mi_m0846/is_8_23/ai_114749468 (accessed December 10, 2007).

11. Susan S. Lang, "Big Portions Influence Overeating as Much as Taste, Even When the Food Tastes Lousy," Cornell University, November 9, 2005, http://www.cals.cornell.edu/cals/public/comm/news/archive/popcorn-pigs.cfm.

12. Brennan et al., "Incidence of adverse events and negligence in hospitalized patients: results of the Harvard Medical Practice Study I," *New England Journal of Medicine* 324 (1991): 370-376.

Section Five: Take Care of Business

1. Susan O'Doherty, *Getting Unstuck Without Coming Unglued* (New York: Seal Press, a division of Perseus Books, 2007.

2. Kevin Hogan, *The Psychology of Persuasion* (New York: Pelican, 1996).

3. Alan Shelton, *Transforming Burnout* (Tacoma, WA: Vibrant Press, 2007).

4. Paivi Leino-Arjas, "Predictors and Consequences of Unemployment Among Construction Workers: Prospective Cohort Study," *British Medical Journal*, September 4, 1999. FindArticles.com, http://findarticles.com/p/articles/mi_m0999/is_7210_319/ai_56000011 (accessed December 10, 2007).

Section Six: Trust God

1. Debra Williams, D.D. "Scientific Research of Prayer: Can the Power of Prayer Be Proven?" *Plim Report* 8, no. 4 (1999), http://www.plim.org/PrayerDeb.htm.

2. Ibid.

3. This research is posted at http://www.SpiritualEnterprise.org.